ARISTOTLE: *A Contemporary Appreciation*

ARISTOTLE

A CONTEMPORARY APPRECIATION

Henry B. Veatch

Indiana University Press   Bloomington & London

Published in Canada by Fitzhenry & Whiteside Limited,
Don Mills, Ontario

Manufactured in the United States of America

Library of Congress Cataloging in Publication Data

Veatch, Henry Babcock.
    Aristotle: a contemporary appreciation.

    Bibliography: p. 200
    1. Aristoteles.   I. Title.
B485. V4   185   73-15280
ISBN 0-253-30890-9   0-253-20174-8 (pbk)

To Francis Parker and Timothy Rhodes
Aristotelians hopefully, friends certainly

Contents

ARISTOTLE: *A Contemporary Appreciation*

Chapter I

Aristotle Redivivus

Poor Aristotle! Having for so many centuries been a dominant force, if not the dominant force, in Western philosophy and in Western culture generally, he now reminds one rather of an enormous stuffed dinosaur. He is not exactly extinct, but he seems hardly to be alive philosophically any more. In consequence, like nearly all dinosaurs, as well as like countless dead philosophers, Aristotle would seem to be reduced to little more than a great, hulking museum piece in the history of Western culture. Classical scholars still translate him and edit his texts; and of course philosopher-historians and historians of ideas continue to write learned books about him; yes, even philosophers themselves—at least during their childhood in the profession—usually find themselves taken around by one of their elders on a tour of the museums of Western philosophy, where they are almost certain to find old Aristotle prominently displayed in an enormous glass case.

Rather than approach Aristotle in this way, why may we not treat him as if he were a contemporary philosopher, like, say, a Wittgenstein, or a Russell, or a Heidegger, or maybe even a Marx, Marcuse, or Sartre? True, these latter are either still alive, or only recently dead, whereas Aristotle is so long dead as perhaps to seem never to have lived at all. Likewise, in what he has written Aristotle nowhere speaks—or at least not in so many words—to current issues like dialectical materialism, or linguistic analysis, or phenomenological reduction, or whatever. Instead, his talk is all about Plato, or Anaxagoras, or Parmenides, or Democritus. How then, is it possible for a thinker of such a totally bygone era to be regarded as a philosopher seriously to be reckoned with today?

There is one rather odd, if not actually impertinent, reason why Aristotle might conceivably be resurrected and made to do duty as a contemporary philosopher right in our very midst, and almost before we know it. For is it not a singular coincidence that in the confusion worse confounded of what we might call our contemporary youth culture, any number of young people today have begun to insist that they are "turned off" by the entire range of modern science and technology? Not only that, but they would not hesitate to throw out, along with science, the whole philosophical and cultural superstructure that has been erected over our increasingly frenzied and uncritical cults of science and technology as they have been developing over the last three hundred years. Now the irony is that the very rise of so-called modern science and modern philosophy was originally associated—certainly in the minds of men like Galileo and Descartes—with a determined repudiation of Aristotle: it was precisely his influence which it was thought necessary to destroy, root and branch, before what we now know as science and philosophy in the modern mode could get off the ground. Accordingly, could it be that as so many of us today are turning our backs so bitterly on all the heretofore boasted achievements of modern culture, we might find ourselves inclined, perhaps even compelled, to return to the Aristotelianism that both antedated and was considered antithetical to the whole modern experiment in knowledge and in living?

Doubtless, to some even the hint of such a return would seem a call to inhabit once more a geocentric universe and a world of final causes where light bodies would tend toward the periphery and heavy bodies toward the center. Be reassured, however. The argument of this present book that Aristotle can and ought to be treated as a contemporary philosopher need not carry with it any such obscurantist implications at all.

At the same time, given a determination to treat Aristotle not as a mere bygone hero of our cultural past, but rather as what William James might call "a live option" in current philosophy, one must be careful not to misconstrue the following brief account of Aristotle's life and influence. It is not an account whose purpose is simply to fix Aristotle's place in history; instead it is intended to remind us of just who and what this man is who we claim should once again become a dominant force on the contemporary philosophical scene.

Aristotle's Life and Subsequent Influence

Aristotle was born in 384 B.C. in the small Greek town of Stagira in Macedonia, slightly to the east of the modern city of Salonika, and so later came to be known as "the Stagirite." He was the son of the court physician to one of the predecessors of the famous and terrible Philip of Macedon. In fact, it may have been due to his family association with the royal house of Macedonia that he later was appointed tutor to Philip's son, Alexander the Great. However, Aristotle's own serious philosophical formation must have begun long before, in the year 367, when he went to Athens to become a member of Plato's renowned school, the Academy. There Aristotle remained for twenty years in the close association of the circle of students and friends who had gathered around Plato. Nor must Aristotle's later sharply-stated philosophical differences from his master lead us to forget his profound devotion and loyalty to

Plato. Indeed, some years after Plato's death, in what Sir Ernest Barker has described as "some memorable elegiac verses," Aristotle wrote of Plato, "he was a man whom the bad have not even the right to praise—the only man, or the first, to show clearly by his own life and by the reasonings of his discourses, that to be happy is to be good." [1]

After Plato's death in 347, Aristotle left the Academy, in part, no doubt, because he was unhappy over the choice of Plato's successor. Nevertheless, his departure from the Academy did not mean a severing of ties with his associates there. On the contrary, accompanied by a friend from the Academy, Xenocrates, who later became himself the head of the Academy, Aristotle crossed the Aegean to Asia Minor, where he and Xenocrates formed an association with two other Platonists at Assos. Some three years later Aristotle left Assos and went to Mytilene on the island of Lesbos. There Aristotle is reputed to have conducted much of his research in biology, particularly marine biology. And it was also in Mytilene that Aristotle is supposed to have received the invitation from Philip to come to Pella, the capital of Macedonia, to tutor Philip's son, Alexander, then a boy of twelve. This close association of a preeminent philosopher with so preeminent a future military leader, particularly during the latter's formative years, has given rise throughout the centuries to endless speculation as to just what Aristotle's influence on the young Alexander must have been during the six years (342–336) that he remained in Pella as Alexander's tutor. Unhappily, such speculation has never been superseded by anything like knowledge.

In any case, by 336 Aristotle had left Pella and returned to Athens for what has sometimes been called the third major phase in his life. In Athens he founded a school of his own, the Lyceum, which was hard by the Academy, the latter then under the direction of Xenocrates. But the times were troubled in Athens, and throughout the entire Greek world. For Alexander was not only extending his conquests, but through his governors and proconsuls bearing down heavily on the already conquered city-states of Hellas. Accordingly, when news reached Athens in 323 of Alexander's death, the patriotic faction seized power and attempted to throw off the Macedonian yoke. Aristotle naturally became highly suspect on account of his earlier connections with Alexander, and was forced to go into exile. In exile the next year (322), Aristotle died and was buried at Chalcis in Euboea, not far from Athens.

At least as interesting as the story of Aristotle's philosophical activity and associations during his own lifetime, is the story of the incredible ups and downs of Aristotle's philosophical influence after his death. For one thing, only by the merest chance, if not actually through divine providence, has the corpus of Aristotle's writings survived at all. For after Aristotle's death, his library, including his own treatises, passed into the hands of Theophrastus, Aristotle's friend and successor in the Lyceum. Theophrastus in turn bequeathed the library to the son of one of Aristotle's friends in Assos; and that man—at least according to a well-attested story—fearing that the books might be seized for the royal library at Pergamum hid the manuscripts in an underground cellar or cave. So effectively were they hidden, however, that not only was the royal library frustrated but the books themselves remained lost for over a hundred years. Finally, they were dug up, and, after passing through various hands, eventually taken to Rome, where they were catalogued and edited by one Andronicus of Rhodes in the first century B.C.

In the course of time, Rome itself, as we all know, went into a decline and fall, and with it the entire ancient world. Aristotle's writings were scattered and lost, and his philosophy fell into almost total eclipse. Happily, though, his work had in the meanwhile penetrated to the Arab world, where his philosophy came to be both enthusiastically and perceptively pursued by many Arab thinkers and scholars. It is to the Arabs that Western culture is ultimately indebted for the survival of Aristotelian philosophy. Throughout the entire period of the so-called Dark Ages in Europe the only works of Aristotle known in the West were certain of his logical treatises. Then came the Crusades and increasing contact with the Arab world; finally there was ushered in what Kenneth Clark has called "the great thaw" of the celebrated twelfth century revival of learning. Soon there began a veritable retransmission of Aristotle's writings back into the West, and with the retransmission there arose a determined and unremitting effort to get everything of Aristotle's translated into medieval Latin. Accompanying this, there also began that incredible flowering of Scholastic philosophy in the thirteenth century, which carried right on through the fourteenth and fifteenth centuries as well, a flowering of which Aristotle's writings were at once the seed and perhaps the nutriment as well. It became customary throughout the Scholastic period simply to refer to Aristotle as "the Philosopher"; and it was left to Dante to sum up what was really the conviction of the entire Middle Ages when he characterized Aristotle as no less than "the master of those who know."

Came the Renaissance, however, and Aristotle, far from being an ancient author clamoring to be rediscovered and reborn, was instead someone who had already been rediscovered and reborn over two centuries before. Even worse, having come to be closely associated with that very Scholasticism in philosophy upon which the men of the Renaissance were heaping scorn and derision, Aristotle went into a decline almost directly proportionate to the soaring reputations of nearly all other classical authors. With the rise of the new science of the Renaissance, there also sprang up a new kind of philosophy that was certainly alien, if not actually antithetical, to the whole Aristotelian outlook and account of the world. True, there was no sudden demise of Aristotle in the Renaissance, or even immediately thereafter. Besides, once launched on its Counter-Reformation, the Roman Church, in its seeming resolve to learn nothing and to forget nothing authoritatively, required that Aristotle should serve as one of the very cornerstones of its philosophical curriculum. But if not an actual life in death, this continued life of Aristotle within the more or less dogmatic confines of the Church was certainly a life lived largely outside the mainstream of modern Western philosophy. And with the recent seeming collapse into anarchy of almost the entire intellectual tradition of the Church, Aristotle appears to have pretty much ceased to count for much philosophically—at least not on the contemporary scene. True, classical scholars have been zealous to preserve and comment on him in their purely scholarly way. Yet to so preserve Aristotle as a historical figure is really to embalm him as a philosopher. How, then, at this time of his lowest ebb philosophically, can Aristotle be said to be ripe for a philosophical revival that once more could return him to the philosophical scene in a veritable high tide of philosophical significance?

How Readable and Intelligible Are the Texts of Aristotle?

There is another disability from which Aristotle suffers that would seem seriously to militate against any return on his part to high philosophical relevance—a largely literary and linguistic disability. In fact, the question can fairly be asked, how can Aristotle so much as speak to us any more? It is not merely a case, when he did speak, of his having spoken and written in Attic Greek of the fourth century B.C., which is no longer a living language and which even as a dead language has been largely relegated to the ill-funded and ill-kept preserve of a few classical scholars. No, for even those very writings of Aristotle which have come down to us from the ancient world, and which for several centuries now we have been reading in Latin or Italian or French or English or German translations—even these writings were not those that could in any sense be called the properly published writings of Aristotle. Instead, they were class-room exercises or lecture notes which either Aristotle himself prepared, or which his students must have jotted down in the course of their instruction in the Lyceum. Is it any wonder, then, that what have reached us of such mere school exercises and notes give every impression of being abbreviated, crabbed, often disconnected, and at times downright unintelligible?

From the ancient world we have Cicero's word that the rhetorical brilliance and literary excellence of the more regularly published writings of Aristotle rivaled even Plato's *Dialogues*. We must take his word for it, for all of Aristotle's formal writings have been lost. Our only access to Aristotle today is through what any present-day professor would certainly regard as singularly disadvantaged materials, his own or his students' notes. It scarcely is surprising that poor Aristotle seems no longer to speak to us with very clear or steady voice; the voice is not even always intelligible.

It is possible, of course, that even today someone—yes, even someone who has never before turned a page of Aristotle—might pick up, say, the Oxford translations of the *Metaphysics* or the *Physics*, or the remarkable English renderings of the *Ethics* and *Politics* in the Loeb Library, and be struck by those frequent luminous judgments and comments of engaging sound sense that stud the texts of Aristotle even in translation. The only trouble is that such evidence of Aristotle's wise judgment and sage observation are unhappily buried in passages whose general tenor is incomprehensible, and whose over-all argument is baffling. As a result, the initial experience of reading Aristotle, however sustained and determined it may be, is often like not seeing the woods for the trees.

Still, mere difficulty of text in Aristotle or any other philosopher could be irrelevant to the question of whether he can speak to us, and do it in a way to make us sit up and take serious philosophical notice. The current philosophical scene is dominated by two figures, Martin Heidegger and Ludwig Wittgenstein. Consider the experience in store for anyone who chances to take a first look at a page in the work of either one. "Gibberish, and pompous gibberish at that!," one might well blurt out at first reading a page of Heidegger. As for Wittgenstein, what he says is not apparent gibberish, but one might still be utterly baffled, not so much as to what he was saying, but rather as to what possible point there might be in his or in anyone else's ever saying it. Yet such difficulties have not deterred thousands upon thousands of students in Germany, England, and America, from rushing after one or the other of these two latter-day philosophical piedpipers. What's more, they will spend hours and days and weeks puzzling over what Heidegger could have meant in this passage, or Wittgenstein in that. To a cynic, indeed, it might almost seem as if any truly living and vibrant philosophy must thrive directly in proportion to the opacity and even perversity of the texts in which it is written.

Aristotle's Present Claim to Fame as a Philosopher of Common Sense

May we not, then, simply take for granted that any difficulties with Aristotle's texts need not be a bar to his becoming once more a genuinely live option in philosophy? Nor is it to the point to argue that Aristotle has already had his day in philosophy. Indeed, of all philosophers Aristotle might be considered as one singularly adept at being in and out of fashion. Thus in addition to his revival among the Arabs, we have already seen how he once had his day among the Greeks, and then, lo!, some 1,500 years later, suddenly came into his own again among the medievals! What, then, is to prevent his becoming fashionable once again, now in the last decades of the twentieth century? Or if that would push things too fast, how about the twenty-first century for our Aristotle *redivivus?*

The proper question, though, is not so much "Why not?" as "Why so?" What is it that Aristotle has to say philosophically that is so decidedly worth listening to, and particularly now. The answer is so elementary as to seem, initially, either question-begging or implausible. It is simply that, on the basis of our common sense, most of us would take to be the case what Aristotle in his philosophy straightforwardly affirms actually is the case. To put it another way, Aristotle is, *par excellence*, the philosopher of common sense. Unfortunately, the term *common sense* has become so hackneyed as to be comparatively uninformative. In an Aristotelian context it could even be misleading, since there the expression *common sense* has become a standard translation of one of Aristotle's own technical terms in his psychology. Perhaps, then, one might do better to fall back upon one of Abraham Lincoln's oft-quoted pronouncements that accurately sums up what is both the consistent and persistent thrust of Aristotle's philosophy. It is Lincoln's remark that while you can perhaps fool some of the people all of the time, and all of the people some of the time, you can't fool all of the people all of the time. So it is for Aristotle: what to all men everywhere in their saner moments is known to be the truth is, indeed, really the truth.

An Eminent Contemporary Example
of Apparent Philosophical Tomfoolery

But let us consider some examples. Or, more precisely, one more or less extended and rambling example that might perhaps be all things to all people.

To begin with, is there anyone of us who does not recognize that he exists in what, in a perfectly ordinary sense, may be said to be a world of people and things, of earth and sky, of birth and death, of good and evil, of time and change, of beauty and ugliness, of coming to be and passing away, of food and drink, of sunshine and rain, etc., etc.? To be sure, in regard to all such things we are well aware of the ordinary sense in which they are understood, and understood as being and existing; while we may at any moment indulge either our operatic or our surrealistic imaginations, we still do not normally mistake such fantasies for reality—unless, of course, we are bent on qualifying ourselves for the madhouse. Thus while we can picture, say, an abandoned wagon wheel sprouting like a rose, or a bare-breasted woman suckling the Empire State Building, it is such things we say that dreams are made of (albeit not necessarily Shakespearean dreams).

In brief, then, our human common sense—or if one would prefer a more old-fashioned term, our natural light of reason—tends not either generally or in the long run to be deceived between dream and reality. However, what goes for our common sense seems not always to go for our scientific or philosophical sense. In those realms, it sometimes seems that almost anything goes. After all, surrealism is not just an art form but a philosophy as well; some would even say a serious philosophy. But it may be a bit unfair, no less to philosophy than to human nature, to cite André Breton as an example of the incredibilities to which our human philosophic sense may sometime lead us. Let's use Bertrand Russell, a more reputable example, and more particularly Bertrand Russell on the subject of Napoleon.

It may be recalled that in one of his more sophisticated philosophical essays Russell asks what we may properly be said to mean when we use the name *Napoleon*. "We commonly imagine," says Russell, "when we use a proper name, that we mean one definite entity, the particular individual who was called 'Napoleon.' " Nevertheless, it is not necessarily true that we mean any such thing; and more properly, as Russell would think, we ought not to mean any such thing. For really, Napoleon, instead of being "one definite entity," who "remained strictly identical from birth to death," is more properly to be regarded as "a complicated series of occurrences, bound together by causal laws." Thus "in the case of a proper name,

> what [the name] means is a series of occurrences bound together by causal laws of that special kind that makes the occurrences taken together constitute what we call one person, or animal or thing, in case the name applies to an animal or thing instead of to a person. Neither the word nor what it means is one of the ultimate indivisible constituents of the world. In language there is no direct way of designating one of the ultimate brief existents that go to make up the collections we call things or persons. If we want to speak of such existents—which hardly happens except in philosophy—we have to do it by means of some elaborate phrase, such as 'the visual sensation which occupied the center of my field of vision at noon on January 1, 1919.' Such ultimate simples I call 'particulars'.[2]

Now ask yourself: in what sense can one possibly give credence to what Russell is saying? Can one accept the fact really—and not merely entertain it as but a fanciful philosophical theory—that a person such as Napoleon, or the tree which I see outside my

Russell

window, or the hand which I hold up before my eyes, is not really one identical thing at all, being only a "complicated series of occurrences bound together by causal laws"? Surely, this is fantastic!

True, one may know how Russell arrived at such a theory, and what arguments he used in support of it. For one thing, when we reflect on the matter a little, it is only too obvious that the existence and character of any material object—a table, a man, a tree, or what not—which we may think we know with certainty, is nonetheless open to doubt. The table which I see in front of me might turn out to be an hallucination. Similarly, if I think the table to be most certainly brown in color and smooth of surface, I have only to consider that, seen in a different light, the color will differ; and examined under a microscope, the surface will appear rough rather than smooth. So Russell concludes, our supposed knowledge of the existence of a material object like the table and of its various features turns out to be not a true knowledge at all. Instead, if I want to fix upon something that I can know with certainty, something that affords me a knowledge so reliable as to be impossible to doubt, then I must reflect that while my knowledge of the table which I fancy that I see before me may well be mistaken, I cannot possibly be mistaken as to my now having just the particular experience that I do have as I look at the table: the sense datum or sense presentation that constitutes my visual experience at this moment is really and indubitably experienced, whether the supposed table as a material object is there or not.

Of course, one might at first suppose that while in all strictness what I am presented with in my experience are not material objects at all, but only sense data, still I should be able to infer the existence and character of the object from these data of my experience. So Russell himself thought at an earlier period of his philosophy. Unfortunately, when he came to determine just what sort of an inference might lead one from sense data to material objects, he found that no such inference, be it either deductive or inductive, could ever be legitimated.

Not being able to understand how in our human knowledge we could get from presented sense data to ordinary material objects existing in the world, Russell simply decided to forget about material objects and to make do with sense data alone. As should be already apparent from his discussion of Napoleon, rather than think of Napoleon as one definite entity who remains one and the same identical individual from birth to death, Russell insists that we should instead think of Napoleon as a "complicated series of occurrences bound together by causal laws," or, as he sometimes put it in other connections, Napoleon is no more than "a logical construction out of sense data."

Such, then, in brief is Russell's argument for what might be called the elimination of material objects from the world altogether, and their replacement with mere sense data. In fact, in Russell's own terminology, material objects are not among "the ultimate furniture of the world" at all, but only such momentary "particulars," as patches of color, sounds, tastes, smells, etc. That is his position. All the same, do we and can we really believe it? Supposing that we have followed Russell's argument for his position step by step—and as a philosophical argument it is a brilliant performance—can we really buy it? Intellectually perhaps we can, but commonsensically must it not strike us as simply unbelievable, not to say fantastic?

Aristotle's Appeal to Common Sense as an Antidote to the Alienations of both Modern Science and Modern Philosophy

"Fantastic!" is surely the sort of judgment that Aristotle would have leveled at a theory like Russell's! Indeed, the justification for our having taken so much time in a book on Aristotle to sketch out a particular philosophical theory of Russell's lies precisely in the fact that the latter can serve as a touchstone to bring out what is most distinctive about the character and temper of Aristotle's philosophy. Although Aristotle never read Russell, he certainly had read any number of his fellow Greek philosophers, who had propounded theories no less fantastic than Russell's. And to all such, Aristotle's consistent reaction was that any philosophical view that appeared patently to fly in the face of the common sense judgment of mankind simply could not be true. Not that you could not find many men who might be taken in by it for much of the time; and perhaps even all men might be taken in for some of the time; but with a view like Russell's you just could not fool all of mankind all of the time!

This is not to say, of course, that Aristotle would have simply rejected Russell's position out of hand just because it goes counter to common sense. On the contrary, as a philosopher, he would feel obliged to examine the Russellian evidence and arguments in support of his position and to show precisely how and where they had gone astray. In fact, that sort of thing formed a large part of Aristotle's philosophical activity—*e.g.,* in showing what was wrong with the Parmenidean arguments that all change was impossible; or with Plato's arguments that there could be no such things as men except as they participated in that perfect and immutable form of Man himself, or no beautiful things except as they participated in the Beautiful itself; or with Heraclitus' contention that since all things were changing, it was impossible for anything ever to be anything, or to have any determinate nature and character at all. In all such cases Aristotle recognized the need to meet his philosophical opponents more or less on their own grounds, and to weigh their arguments as carefully as possible in preparation for trying to answer and refute them. Still, his initial suspicions in regard to any and all scientific or philosophical views were most likely to be prompted if it seemed that such views could not in the long run stand the test of the sound common sense of mankind in general.[3]

With this we would hope that we might have won at least an initial tolerance for our contention that Aristotle is a philosopher who deserves to be listened to in the present-day in the same way as one of our more challenging contemporaries. For modern culture, no less in its science than in its philosophy, has proved to be, if not no respecter of persons, then certainly no respecter of the common sense of persons, or of what we might better call the naturally informed judgment of mankind. Could this perhaps be at least one of the causes of the unhappy foundering of contemporary culture which we are witnessing on every hand? For who of us does not experience a kind of schizophrenia, or perhaps even a kind of alienation, between the everyday world in which we live as human beings among other human beings, and the world as it is represented to us by our contemporary scientists and philosophers?

So far as philosophy is concerned, we might consider the example of Russell to be not untypical. Surely, Russell could scarcely have denied that the world which he believed in as a philosopher was hardly the world which he lived in as a human being. Thus imagine Russell shaking hands with a friend, or haranguing a mass meeting in condemnation of the U.S. military involvement in Vietnam. Doubtless in such circumstances he might have stuck to his philosophical conviction that any statements he might make concerning the people and things in the immediate situation confronting him were reducible by definitions-in-use to statements only about sense data and not about people and things at all. Yet no less doubtless would it appear that even Russell could hardly have been so committed to his own philosophy as to assume in his attitudes and behavior, even if not in his thoughts, that the people and things that he was having to do with were but so many groupings and series of sense data.

What goes for modern philosophy generally would certainly go for modern science as well: the scientific universe of modern physics, astronomy, and biology is scarcely the world which as human beings we are conscious of ourselves as living in, or as interacting with, or as upon occasion either enjoying or suffering. Indeed, in the earliest days of the great scientific revolution, we find Galileo in the seventeenth century simply excluding from the physical universe all so-called secondary qualities, and treating as being real only the primary qualities of figure, size, motion, quantity, location, etc. Even today it is still insisted that "molecules have no color, atoms make no noise, electrons have no taste, and corpuscles do not even smell." [4] Now it has come to be recognized that spatial and temporal relations as we experience them are quite different from physical space and time as they are in themselves. Not only that, but the latter day scientific theories and fundamental hypotheses, through which whole ranges of scientific data come to be ordered and related to one another, are such as to leave the face of nature quite unpicturable to us. As hypotheses they are sometimes said not to be derived or induced from the empirical data at all; nor are they even, some would say, subject to verification or falsification through experience—or at least not in any very obvious sense. Little wonder, then, that the universe which the scientist acknowledges in his professional capacity turns out to be not at all that everyday world which as a human being he never doubts himself to be a part of, when, say, he sits down to have a drink with his friends or casts his ballot in an election or walks up the stairs in the morning to his office or laboratory.

All this being so, why should we not at least listen to Aristotle for a time—Aristotle whose basic philosophical endeavor is to try to bring us back from the realms alike of surrealistic fantasy and of our no less elaborate and involuted scientific and philosophical imaginations, and to anchor us once again to those everyday realities to which the sober judgment and common sense of all mankind would appear to bear such indefeasible testimony. Can such a thing be done? Is such a philosophical program any longer defensible? Let us hear Aristotle out and we shall see.

Chapter II

Physics: The Nature of
Things Physical

"What are the major sorts or varieties of things in the universe?"
"What are the basic kinds of entities?" Or, to borrow Russell's
phrase, "What types of things make up 'the ultimate furniture of
the world?'" Questions of this sort, although Aristotle does not
pose them in these words, may nevertheless serve as preliminaries
to what he called "physics" or an over-all account of nature and of
the natural world. Besides, they are common-sense questions as
well. Indeed, all of us can readily imagine ourselves as giving more
or less common-sense answers to such common-sense questions.
"Well," we might say, "the world is made up of people and things
of various kinds. More specifically, perhaps, there are all sorts of
inanimate objects, as well as countless varieties of plants and of
animals—fish in the sea, birds in the air, and beasts of the field."
One is even reminded of the old saying about fish and fowl and
good red herring.

While we would doubtless recognize any such classification to
be overly simple, we might nonetheless suppose that greater
sophistication would lead to a classification that was only more
elaborate, rather than to one that was basically different in principle.

Yet Aristotle would insist upon a type of classification that would be somewhat different in principle, while nevertheless not departing from common sense, or from what all of us would acknowledge to be commonsensical on the basis of our everyday experience. Surely, the things of the world, be they fish or fowl, all have size; they can only be located either here or there; and at different times various characteristics or qualities must pertain to them. Not only that, but most things are sometimes active, in the sense that they may be said to be doing something; and sometimes passive, in the sense that various things are being done to them or are happening to them. Likewise they stand in various relations one to another. And so on.

Is not, though, the size of a thing at least something? So the relations in which it stands to other things are also something. And where a thing is—its location—is that not something too? Similarly, what it is doing, its activities, not to mention the times when it engages or does not engage in such activities—these, too, are no less real; and in this sense, although it may be stretching the meaning of the terms *things* or *entities* or *beings* to use them in such a connection, surely times and places and relations and actions are all in their own way something or other, and hence beings, things—call them what you will—entities of their own characteristic sort.

With this, then, begins to emerge Aristotle's celebrated doctrine of the categories, the *categories* being the ultimate headings under which anything and everything in the world can be classified—that is to say, the basic kinds of things, or the fundamental varieties of entities that may be said to comprise the ultimate furniture of the world. In other words, the sense of the doctrine of the categories is that anything whatever, or at least anything physical, any denizen of the physical world, must be either the *quantity* or size or amount of something, or else a *quality* of something, or the *place* or location of something, or the *relation* of something to something else, or the *action* or *passion* of something, or the *time* at which it occurs, etc. Nor must one forget still another category, which is the most important one of all—that "something" which a quantity is said to be the quantity or size of, or a quality the quality of, or a place the place of, or an action the action of. Aristotle's term—or rather the standard translation of the Aristotelian term—to designate simply that which any such quantities or qualities or actions or whatnot may be said to be in or of is the famous term *substance*. In other words, a quantity, for instance, simply could not be or exist without its being the quantity of something—that is, of a substance. Could there possibly be such a thing as simply a two-and-a-half foot length, without there being anything that was of this length or had this length? Or better, take something like walking. Could you have walking—just walking all by itself—without there being anything that did or does the walking? Or what about virtue? Could there be just virtue, without there being anything at all that could be said to have such virtue, or that could be said thus to be virtuous? In sum, all categories of things other than substances have the decisive feature of only being able to be or to exist in substance. They are, in the literal sense of the term, *accidents* (from *ad* (to) - *cadere* (fall) of substance).

Accordingly, Aristotle's categorical classification of all of the different types and kinds of things that there are or that can be in the physical world may be briefly summed up in the simple, evident principle: anything whatever must be either a substance or an accident of a substance. Returning to the classification of things as either fish or fowl or good red herring, we can now see that on Aristotle's scheme, fish and fowl and herring are all in the category of substance. But clearly, there are all sorts of other things in the world. For instance, what about the smell of the herring? Inseparable though it may be from the fish, or at least from certain kinds of fish, the smell is still not to be confused with the fish itself: a herring's smell is but a feature or quality of the herring, not the herring! And so likewise, the size of a thing—in this case, the herring—is certainly something distinguishable from the herring. Or as Aristotle would put it, the size of a thing is in the category of quantity, not in that of substance. Again, the question of where the herring is in the sea would be one of its place or location, as contrasted with a question as to its size (quantity) or as to its odor (quality). Suppose, too, as still another alternative, that the question were one of what the herring was doing, namely, swimming. This time the thing in question, the fish's swimming about, would be in the category of action.

Perhaps, though, simply to quote a short passage written by a biologist of a generation or so ago would bring out at once the common-sense import and the common-sense basis of the doctrine of the categories:

> The botanist describing a new plant assumes implicitly, that he is dealing with a real, self-contained entity forming the subject of his description, and thus assumes it to be a *substance.* He measures his specimen and gives its *dimensions.* He describes its colour, its shape, the character of its leaves and flowers, in a word its *qualitative* or specific attributes. He notes its place in the flora, its *relation* to other organisms. He mentions the *date* on which he discovered it, the spot in which it grew, its *position*, its *activities,* and the *effect exerted on it* by other living things. All of these points appear to him to be necessary and irreducible elements in his description.[1]

In short, what is brought home by a quotation like this is simply the fact that, whether we like it or not, or whether it has ever before occurred to us or not, we cannot help recognizing that anything and everything whatever in the world are bound to be either substances or accidents of substances—that is, either a thing in the sense of a *substance*; or a quality of such a thing; or its size or *quantity*; or perhaps something that that thing is doing (*action*) or something that is being done to it (*passion*); or that thing's *place* or location; or its *position*; or its date or *time*; or possibly a *relation* of that thing to another; and so on. To be sure, it makes little difference whether we accept Aristotle's particular list of categories, whether we add still further categories which Aristotle does not have, or whether we reduce some of those which he does have to others. Rather what is important is that such a rudimentary classification of all things as being either substances or accidents of a substance is, indeed, a "necessary and irreducible" classification of the ultimate furniture of the world. This is simply the way things are; it is an ultimate fact of nature; and it is undeniably attested to simply by our common sense, or by what Bergson once felicitously characterized as *la métaphysique naturelle de l'esprit humain*.

Perhaps we should immediately note, at least in passing, that the mere fact that such a physics or metaphysics should thus commend itself to our common sense as being at once so natural and so obvious as scarcely to seem open to question, by no means implies that this scheme of things would commend itself to the sophisticated philosopher. To Bergson himself it certainly did not so commend itself; and to Russell, to take another example, it was even less commendable. In fact, it even occasioned on Russell's part a caustic quip about "the metaphysics of the stone age to which common sense is due!" Nor did he stop at mere quips, but rather in a celebrated passage he chose to fly jauntily in the face of stone-age metaphysics of common sense as typified by Aristotle:

There is a notion that an instance of walking, as compared with Jones, is unsubstantial, but this seems a mistake. We think that Jones walks, and there could not be any walking unless there was somebody like Jones to perform the walking. But it is equally true that there could be no Jones unless there were something like walking for him to do. The

notion that actions are performed by an agent is liable to the same kind
of criticism as the notion that thinking needs a subject or ego. To say
that it is Jones who is walking is merely to say that the walking in
question is part of the whole series of occurrences which is Jones.
There is no *logical* impossibility in walking occurring as an isolated
phenomenon, not forming part of any such series as we call a
"person." [2]

This rather typical Russellian *pronunciamento* to the effect that
there is no logical impossibility to there being such a thing as
walking without anything doing the walking we must here pass
over in silence. But Russell's very manner and mode of defiance of
Aristotle's doctrine of the categories serves to point up both the
common-sense character of that doctrine and the difficulty of
challenging it, short of seeming to be utterly, if not outrageously,
paradoxical.

⸪ Physical Change: Philosophical Arguments
Against the Very Possibility of Change

Back to physics. As we have already remarked, the fact that the
things of the world must be either substances or accidents of
substance is not something that Aristotle undertakes to establish in
his *Physics* as such. Rather in his eyes the distinctive thing about all
things physical or natural is what we today would probably call
their pervasively "dynamic" character: physics is precisely the
region or domain of change or motion, where things come into
being and pass away, where few things are stationary, but most are
subject to motion from place to place, where many things get larger
or smaller, where they change their features and even their ways,
and where, possibly, nothing can be said to be absolutely the same
from moment to moment.

At the same time, motion and change, however much we may take them for granted simply as a matter of common sense, are not as readily or immediately intelligible as we might suppose. In fact, philosophers, both before and after Aristotle, have been given to making sport of what most of us would probably take to be the simple and obvious fact of change. There just cannot be any such thing, many of them have said. Others have declared that although change is indeed real, it absolutely defies understanding. And still others have insisted that although in one sense change might be said to be both real and intelligible, in another sense it isn't really change at all that is so, but rather something basically different from change and with which change is often confused.

Turning to Aristotle, it might be expected that as is his wont, his initial and basic concern would be to salvage and rehabilitate the common-sense view of change. He does just that in the first three books of the *Physics*, his procedure being to lay bare the underlying principles and causes through which the fact of change may be made at once demonstrable and intelligible. However, in order properly to recognize what Aristotle is here fighting for, we must first consider briefly what Aristotle took himself to be fighting against. Let us attempt a brief and highly stereotyped picture of three philosophical positions in regard to change that are most inimical to common sense. Let us call them somewhat arbitrarily the Heraclitean, the Parmenidean, and the Zenonian or succession view of change.

As to Heraclitus, Aristotle represents him as holding the view that nothing in the world is ever free from change at any time. But then if thing A is constantly in process of change, and if there is not any part or feature of A which is free from change, then it is really impossible for A either to be A, or ever to have been A. For no sooner is such a thing as A presumed to be what it is—namely, A—than it must already have changed and become different, so that it is not and never really was A at all. But the upshot of such a view is simply that nothing ever is anything; nor is it possible ever to know anything as being this rather than that, or as having any determinate nature or character at all. In fact, Aristotle rather humorously characterizes this Heraclitean view of change by recounting an alleged dispute between Heraclitus and his disciple Cratylus. Heraclitus had maintained that it was impossible for a man to step into the same river twice: after all, the river being constantly in flow, how could it be the same river from moment to moment? Cratylus took exception, maintaining against his master that so far from one's ever being able to step into the same river twice, you could not even step into it once!

For Heraclitus the fact of change rendered the whole of nature and the natural world unintelligible. And interestingly enough, when one turns to the Parmenidean view of change, at least as Aristotle understands it, it seems that Parmenides recognized much the same dilemma as Heraclitus: either change or intelligibility, but not both. But whereas Heraclitus was willing to sacrifice intelligibility in order to stick with the fact of change, Parmenides favors an outright denial of the fact of the change in order to maintain intelligibility. For Parmenides was not willing merely to deny that there is change: he propounded arguments to show that change itself is impossible.

In brief, the argument takes shape something like this. If change is to be real, or if there is to be any such thing as change, then that must mean that the real, or that which is, must somehow change. But for anything to change it must become other and different, or it could not be said to have changed at all. For reality, or that which is, or the real, to become different can only mean that it becomes other than real, or unreal. Unfortunately, this lands one in a flat contradiction. To say that the real has changed or has become unreal implies that the situation resulting from such change is one in which the real must be said to be unreal or other than real; or in which that which is must now be recognized as being that which is not: "The real is not real; or that which is is that which is not." Hence Parmenides concludes that all change is impossible because self-contradictory.

A Parmenidean denial of change in favor of intelligibility, however, suggests in its turn a third view of change, which we might call the Zenonian view[3] of change as mere succession. One might readily say that where the notion or concept of change as Parmenides envisages it, seems to get into difficulties and ultimately to generate a self-contradiction is at that point where change is construed as involving the idea of something changing or becoming different. For if anything—any "it," shall we say—changes or becomes different, then it must be said to be no longer what it is: it is, therefore, now a not-it. But why not try to escape this contradiction by simply eliminating the notion of a thing's changing or undergoing change? Instead, why not consider that a given thing is what it is; and then, rather than changing or becoming different, that the thing is simply succeeded by something other and different? Or to express the same point in symbols, rather than to make the mistake of supposing that an A can ever become non-A, why not suppose that A, after existing for a time, simply ceases to be, and then is succeeded by something other than A, say, B. Here there is no contradiction: one does not say that A becomes or is B (that is, non-A); rather one merely says that first A exists, and then is followed or succeeded by B.

Moreover, once one moves from these abstract considerations to the concrete situation of the natural world, one immediately recognizes that succession no less than change is indeed a fact of nature. Lightning, for example, is followed by thunder, or sickness by health, or one day is succeeded by another. Yet we would never say that the lightning itself actually becomes thunder, or sickness health, or one day another. Accordingly, succession is no less a fact of nature than is change.

All the same, let it not be forgotten that so far as common sense goes, change is not to be simply excluded from nature in favor of succession. As we recognize that lightning is followed by thunder, but does not become thunder, no less do we recognize that a man becomes old, that a leaf changes from green to yellow or that a body—the same body—is moved from one place to another. Yet on the Zenonian view of change, all such supposed cases or instances of change must be reduced to instances of succession. For example, rather than to suppose that it is the same leaf that is now green and then changes color and becomes yellow, we should rather need to suppose that first there is a green leaf, which in turn is succeeded by a different leaf that has a yellowish tinge, and this by still another leaf that is more decidedly yellow, until finally there succeeds still a different leaf that is completely yellow.

Indeed, in this Zenonian view of change, in which change is actually eliminated and replaced with the notion of succession, do we not recognize perhaps a prototype of that view to which we have already found Bertrand Russell subscribing in the earlier quoted account of Napoleon? For in denying that there was any strictly identical ego of Napoleon that remained the same from his birth to his death, what Russell was really suggesting was that Napoleon is really nothing but a succession of momentary appearances or a series of occurrences tied together by causal laws—"first a squalling baby, then a boy, then a slim and beautiful youth," etc. And so the Zenonian view of change is found to live again in Bertrand Russell, much as the Heraclitean and Parmenidean views of change also have their contemporary representatives.

Physical Change: Aristotle's Analysis and Defense of It in Terms of the Three Principles of Change

What, now, of Aristotle? Already we have suggested that his stand is that of course there is such a thing as motion or change. This is a fact borne in upon us and upon all men by simply indubitable evidence, whatever the sophisticated arguments of philosophers to convince us that what is seemingly so evident is not really evident at all. Still, these arguments cannot be brushed aside merely on the ground that they go counter to common sense. Rather they must be carefully weighed and rebutted. Or better, the notions of change or motion themselves need to be more thoroughly analyzed, in order to determine what principles are actually involved; and once such principles are clearly recognized and we are able to see just what is requisite for there to be any such thing as change at all, then the Heraclitean and Parmenidean and Zenonian objections may well turn out to be at once harmless and beside the point. Such principles of change Aristotle considers to be three in number, and he calls them *form, matter,* and *privation.* As to form and privation, it is readily understandable what they are and why they should be thought essential to any occurrence or instance of change and motion. For all change must be from something to something else; otherwise nothing could be said to have changed at all and everything would be just the same. To be more specific, though, is it not obvious that any change from something to something else must really be construed as being a change, let us say, from being X to not being X; or vice versa from not being X to being X? Thus the man who was once healthy is now no longer so; or the plant that was once a tiny seedling (*i.e.,* was not tall) has now grown tall; or the water that was cool is now hot, etc.

In other words, by the technical term *form* Aristotle means primarily a specific determination of something. The fact that a thing is this rather than that, that it is blue rather than orange, or that it is here rather than there, or that it is a dog rather than a cat—all of these possible determinations of things are so in virtue of what Aristotle calls forms; or rather the determinations of things simply are forms. For that matter, the categories which were considered in the preceding section are only so many ways in which things may be determinate or have determinate features and characteristics—quantity or quality or substance or place or what not. Accordingly, the categories, considered as a classification of the ways in which things may be determinate, are thus simply a classification of the formal determinations or forms of things.

Returning then to the question of motion or change, since all change must be from something's being thus and so to its not being so, or from its not being so to its being thus and so, Aristotle can quite properly say that among the principles of change must certainly be reckoned form and the privation of form.

However, the third of Aristotle's principles of change, that of matter, is perhaps rather more difficult to grasp. Yet the need for such a principle can be readily seen from the insufficiency of the other two principles. For, strictly speaking, no form can ever change into its opposite or contrary. Take, for example, the color red. Surely, there is nothing that would normally prevent a red object from taking on a different color: a red barn can be painted blue, a red face can turn pale. Yet notice that although a red thing or object can certainly acquire a different color, redness itself cannot, say, become blue. Similarly, as regards size or quantity: a corn plant that was only six inches in height can become six feet high; but six inches as such can never become six feet.

Consequently, if there is to be such a thing as change, there must be a third principle involved other than the two principles of form and privation. In fact, this need of a third principle only serves to point up once more something which we noted earlier in regard to change, as contrasted with succession—that change always involves a something that changes, or a something that undergoes or underlies or sustains the change. What then is this something?

At first, one might be inclined to respond that it must be a substance, in Aristotle's sense, that underlies or undergoes change. Nor would this answer be altogether mistaken. If we hark back again to the doctrine of the categories, as it must always be what Aristotle calls substance that is of a certain size or has a certain quality or is active in various ways or is located here or there, etc., so also it would seem that it would have to be a substance that changes from being of a certain size to being either larger or smaller, or that changes from being in one place to being in another, etc. And sure enough, in the rough and ready examples that we have already used, it would seem definitely to be borne out that the thing-that-changes or the that-which-changes is a substance. For if it is not the size, six inches tall, that changes to six feet tall, but rather the corn plant that has or is of that size that does so, then surely such a thing as a plant is in the category of substance, rather than in that of quantity, or relation, or place, or what not. So also if it is not the color red that becomes pale, but rather a red face that does so, clearly a face is classifiable as a substance rather than as an accident of a substance.

Yet Aristotle does not reckon substance as being the third principle of change; rather this is what he calls *matter*. Why? His basic consideration is that once it be recognized that all change requires that there be a something that changes, it must also be recognized that, in order for it to change, that something must be such as to be able to change or become different. And it is such an ability or capacity or potentiality for being other and different that Aristotle calls matter. It's true that this term is likely to be something of a stumbling block for us today, accustomed as we are to thinking of matter and of material objects as being that which occupies space and has weight, or as having extension and mass, or however we may want to put it. But not so Aristotle. For him matter is simply potentiality; and potentiality, in turn, is always construed as a potentiality for something or other. Thus, in the context of change, that which changes must be something with at least a potentiality for being other and different. In other words, it must be what Aristotle would call a material thing or substance.

And while it is indeed always a substance that changes, it is nevertheless in virtue of its matter or potentiality that it is able to undergo change. Accordingly, it is precisely matter, rather than substance, that is properly to be reckoned as the third principle of change. Or to reach the same conclusion from a slightly different angle, it is Aristotle's view that the substances of the natural world—men, plants, animals, physical bodies, the four elements (earth, air, fire, and water)—are all composite of form and matter; that is to say, in addition to the substantial form that determines a substance like fire, say, to be one kind of a thing or substance rather than some other kind, fire also contains a material component. For fire can change: it can increase or decrease; it can be moved from one place to another; it can even die down and cease to be altogether. Given such an ability or capacity or potentiality to be other and different from that which at any given moment it actually is, fire is not just form alone, not just something determinate, but also, in Aristotle's sense, something material—that is, it has a potentiality to take on other forms and other determinations from those which it presently has.

Moreover, lacking such a material component, fire or any other substance would simply be altogether incapable of change. We have earlier had occasion to note that forms as such do not change: redness as such can never become greenness, however easily that which is red can become green; roundness as such can never be any other shape, even though that which is round may very well come to have a different shape. To take a still different example, human nature—the substantial form of being a man or being human—does not change in any way: it does not become pale or sick; it does not run fast or stand still; nor does it ever grow old and die. Indeed, when a particular man grows old and dies and is no more, we do not for a minute suppose that human nature has therefore changed or ceased to be. Accordingly, without matter the things and substances of the world would never change; and with matter, what must be understood is that any thing or substance in the world, in addition to being what it determinately is at any given moment—that is, in addition to its substantial form and all of the accidental forms as a result of which it is just this kind of a thing with these particular characteristics and determinate features at this particular moment— such a thing is also able or capable of being other and different, of acquiring other forms and determinate features. And it is this potentiality for change, which substances in the natural world have, that is their matter, and as a result of which they are said to be material substances.

With this, then, we can perhaps begin to see how the three Aristotelian principles of change are to be projected against the background of the Aristotelian categories, so as to give a kind of over-all picture both of such changes as take place in nature and of how they take place. As Aristotle sees it, changes can occur only within four out of all the categories; that is to say, changes can only be either changes of quantity, or of quality, or of place, or finally changes of substance. Take the example of a particular man; let's say his name is Joe. Of course, Joe is a substance; and as a substance in the natural world, he is a material substance, which means that he has a potentiality for all sorts of forms or determinations other than those which he has at a given moment. Thus Joe might change in size by becoming heavier or lighter, or perhaps even by growing taller or shorter: this would be a change in quantity (in the category of quantity). Or he might change in quality: from being pale, he might become ruddy; from being ignorant, he might become learned; or from being handsome he might become ugly. And of course, as a normal human being, Joe is able to move about from place to place: this would be loco-motion, or change of place. Then finally, like all men, Joe has not always been and will not always be: there was a time when he was born and came into being, and there will be a time when he will die and be no more. Such changes as this last, unlike mere changes of quantity or quality or place, are actual substantial changes, just in the sense that in such cases it is no less than a substance that either comes into being or passes away.

Moreover, in all of these instances of change, the three principles of change are present and operative. For in changes of quantity or of quality or of place, it is the matter of the substance that both has a certain determination in respect to quantity or place, and at the same time has a potentiality for a different determination in either quantity or quality or place; and in the case of each of the three types of change, the two formal determinations stand opposed to one another as contraries, or as form and privation. Further, what happens in the process of the change itself is that the matter or material substance which thus underlies the change simply loses the formal determination it had—be it a determination as to quantity or quality or place—and takes on another and different such formal determination.

Likewise, but also rather more radically, when it comes to substantial change, as contrasted with the accidental changes just mentioned, it is the matter and matter alone that has to be said to lose one substantial form and take on another; in other words, it cannot be a material substance that undergoes the change, as in the case of quantitative and qualitative changes and changes of place, for it is the substance itself that now comes into being or passes away. Hence, it is just matter alone, or what Aristotle calls prime matter, that first is determined by one substantial form, and then as a result of the change comes to be determined by another and different such form. For instance, for water to change from being warm to being hot is one thing; but for something that has the substantial form of water to become a different substance altogether, say air—in such a case nothing underlies or can be said to undergo such a change other than prime matter itself or the pure potentiality of becoming another and different substance.

Granted, then, that in all cases of motion or change, be it substantial or accidental change, the three principles of form, matter, and privation are operative, one must go on to ask how is it that Aristotle supposes that a clear recognition of these principles will dispose of the Heraclitean, Parmenidean, and Zenonian difficulties in regard to change? The answer should already be evident. For Heraclitus' difficulty, as we have seen, arose from the fact that, not understanding how forms as principles of determinacy and intelligibility could ever change, he simply denied that in a world of change there could be any forms or principles of determinacy of any kind. Moreover, he frankly accepted the consequences of such a position by admitting that, given a universal flux and change, nothing could ever even so much as be what it is, much less be known to be either this or that or anything else. To this Aristotle's response is that the mere fact of changes—even of changes everywhere and all of the time in the natural world—certainly does not preclude things from having formal determinations or from being determinately this, that, or the other. On the contrary, a contrariety of formal determinations (what Aristotle designates simply as a form and its privation) is present in every instance or type of change, be it a substantial change or a mere accidental change of either quantity or quality or place. Hence on Aristotle's account of change there is no incompatibility between nature and the things of nature being intelligible by means of their formal determinations, and at the same time of their being constantly subject to change and flux.

On the other hand, as against the Zenonian view which would eliminate change in favor of succession, on the ground that forms and formal determinations can never change but at most can only succeed one another, Aristotle's reply is that in one sense this is perfectly true: forms as such cannot change or become different; however, in the concrete changes that are in fact going on in nature all of the time and that are such an obvious fact of our experience, it is not the formal principles of things that undergo such changes, but rather matter and the material components that are invariably a part of any and all natural substances. In other words, the Zenonian difficulties in regard to change result from an effort to understand motion and change by means of principles that are simply insufficient.

The Aristotelian answer to Parmenides is not basically different from his answer to the Zenonians: it involves the recognition of matter as a principle of change. Thus Parmenides' difficulty turned on his not understanding how the real, or that which is, could ever change or become different, since then it would have to be pronounced to be unreal, or to be that which is not. To this Aristotle's answer is that the real is not just an affair of formal determinations or even of one simple form, namely, the Real. No, the reality of matter and of potentiality must be recognized along with that of form; and matter, unlike form, is just that which is capable of being other and different. Hence if to be real involves more than simply being determinate through the one form, Reality, then there is no reason why what is real could not change without having for that reason to be pronounced unreal. No, for that which is, or is real in the sense of being only potentially determinate with respect to some form or formal determination, can perfectly well change, in the sense of acquiring such a formal determination without thereby becoming unreal.

What Change or Motion Is: Its Definition and Its Causes

May not this Aristotelian account of change, in terms of its three principles, and particularly in terms of the indispensable role of matter in all change, serve somewhat to restore our faith in the common-sense, everyday world of physical nature and physical change? Nor is that all. Aristotle caps his discussion with a somewhat enigmatic but still very pregnant statement of definition as to just what change is. Perhaps, though, *definition* is the wrong word, for what Aristotle might more properly be thought to be doing is trying to specify or to fix the peculiar sort of being or reality, or the distinctive and yet unusual ontological status, which change might be considered to have in the universe. After all, the categories, as we have seen, were supposed to be a classification of all of the major kinds of things or entities that there are in the world. Yet what about change? There is no category so listed among the others; nor could anyone very readily see how change or motion could be reckoned under any of the categories that Aristotle does list. Certainly change is not a quality of anything, or a substance, or a location, or a relation, or what not. Yet surely it is something, and not nothing at all. In fact, that is the whole point of Aristotle's defense of change against its detractors among the philosophers. How then does it happen that change or motion has no place among Aristotle's categories?

The answer to this question will no doubt be seen as already implicit in what has been said thus far. The categories, as we have noted, are really forms; they represent the various ways or modes in which the things of the world are definite and determinate, as substances, or as quantities or qualities or actions or relations or what not of substances. But change or motion just isn't determinate in this way. Quite the contrary, a necessary principle of all change is the principle of matter or potentiality; and matter as such is nothing determinate, being only potential with respect to determinations; it, matter, is neither this nor that, but is only able to become this or that. Moreover, it is no less than the very becoming, or the progress or transition from being only potentially thus and so to being actually thus and so, that is change or motion.

For instance, a young man who, shall we say, has an obvious talent or aptitude for carpentry or the computer sciences or medicine, but who actually has none of the skills, having just started to learn one of them—he, we might say, as a learner is in process of change, in this case a change in quality, from being unskilled to being skilled. So long as he has only a potentiality for being a doctor, say, but has yet done nothing about learning the art, he is to that extent and in that respect not progressing and hence not changing or developing. On the other hand, once he has learned the art and has actually become a skilled physician, then he is no longer changing either—at least not in this particular respect. Instead, the process of change or development is now over and completed, and he who formerly was only potentially skilled is now actually so.

Or take another, and in some ways a simpler and even cruder example. Suppose that I have in my hand an unstretched rubber band that is three inches long, but capable of being stretched to six inches. So long as it is not being stretched, it obviously is not in process of changing its length. On the other hand, once it has been stretched to six inches and actually is of that length, then it is no longer in process of being stretched and thus of being changed. Hence the change as such is to be located directly in the very process of the rubber band's being stretched—that is, in the very transition from its being only potentially six inches long to its being actually six inches long. Moreover, during the process of change or transition, the rubber band, strictly speaking, is not of any determinate length: it is not three inches long; it is not six inches long; indeed, unless the process of change is stopped or interrupted somewhere along the way, the band as it is being stretched is not of this length or that, but always in between or on the way from one to the other.

Accordingly, Aristotle tries to capture all of these various features of change or motion by characterizing it as simply the fulfilling, or the complet*ing,* or the perfect*ing,* or the actuali*zing* of a thing's potentiality, until that thing actually has become that which it formerly was only potentially. In other words, change is precisely that intermediate condition of a thing between its being only potentially thus and so and its being actually thus and so. Merely having a potentiality does not constitute a change; and once the potentiality has been actualized, the change is then finished; thus it is that very actualizing of a potentiality, or of that which is potential, in so far as it is potential, that is the change.

Aristotle's Doctrine of the Four Causes of Change

Granting, then, that such is what change in the physical world is—the very actualizing of a potentiality—and granting, too, that any such actualizing or realizing of a potentiality must involve at least three principles—matter and a contrariety of formal determinations—that still does not tell us what causes such changes, or actually brings them about. As Aristotle uses the term *principles,* it represents, as it were, the requisite pre-conditions that are necessary if there is to be any such thing as change at all; but for a change actually to occur or take place, there must be something actually to cause that change.

True, Aristotle himself is perhaps none too clear as to how he would have us understand his own distinction between principles and causes. He does suggest that while all causes of change are at the same time principles, not all principles are causes. Perhaps, though, to bring out the peculiar significance of this distinction, we might invoke the modern notion of what may be called necessary, as contrasted to sufficient, conditions of change. In the light of our argument in this chapter thus far, it should be obvious that the three principles of change are certainly necessary if there is to be any change; but even given the presence of these principles, that still is scarcely sufficient to cause a change actually to take place. Thus to recur to our earlier example, it is not merely quite conceivable, but is frequently the case that someone may both be unskilled in a particular art and also have a capacity for acquiring such a skill, and yet do nothing about it: that is to say, the process of change—in this case the learning—just never gets under way.

On the other hand, suppose that our subject does begin to learn, surely his capacity for such learning—what Aristotle would call the matter or potentiality—must continue throughout the process. Remove a man's capacity for learning, even if the learning process be already under way, and the learning will cease. Likewise, as the material principle of change must be there throughout the process of change, so also must the formal principle. After all, the change is a change of the man (material principle) *from* being unskilled (privation) *to* being skilled (formal principle). Hence this formal determination, although it is not actually realized until the process of change is complete, nevertheless is determinative of the entire process, and is so throughout the entire process, and in such a way that without it that particular process of change or development would not be the change or process that it is. In this case it is a process of learning, which on Aristotle's scheme of the categories would be a change in quality; and as such it is not a change in quantity or in place or in substance. Hence the principle of formal determination is a necessary condition of the change, not just at its inception and, so to speak, at its point of departure, but also as a continuing principle that must remain throughout the process of change and as determining the change to be that kind of a change and not some other.

Not so, however, that third principle of change, which Aristotle calls *privation*. For the privation—in this case, being unskilled—is a principle in the sense of being a mere point of departure: it is, to be sure, a necessary prerequisite to there being a process of learning, but it is, as it were, something that is left behind in the process of the man's becoming skilled from having been unskilled.

And so it is that of the three principles of change, only two of them must remain as the continuing necessary conditions of the change, even while the change is going on, whereas the third principle, that of privation, although it is a necessary condition in the sense of being the starting point or point of departure of the change, is not a continuing condition of the process itself. Accordingly, when Aristotle comes to discuss the causes of change, as contrasted with the principles of change, he promptly converts two of his principles into causes, what he calls the *material cause* and the *formal cause*. What he has in mind in doing so is no doubt a consideration more or less of the sort that we have just been discussing, namely, that matter and form continue as necessary conditions of the on-going process of change itself, and are not mere necessary conditions of the change's getting started, or merely requisite as providing its point of departure, as is the case with privation. So it is, then, that for Aristotle matter and form are no less causes than they are principles of change, whereas privation is only a principle and not a cause.

For all of this, however, many of us will doubtless feel somewhat baffled as to why Aristotle considers the matter and the form of a given change to be actual causes of that change. Necessary conditions they certainly are, and perhaps they are necessary conditions in a way in which mere privation is not. But why call them causes? Perhaps it is no more than a terminological difficulty in that Aristotle's term for *cause* in Greek may have had a rather different connotation from that which it has in English. However this may be, it is certainly true that while Aristotle did feel that matter and form needed to be reckoned among the actual causes of change, he recognized at the same time that they were only necessary and not sufficient conditions of any change, and that, of the further conditions that were requisite in any on-going process of change, there were others that needed to be reckoned as being, if not more decisive causes of change, at least as causes of a distinctively different sort.

To bring this out, however, let us again have recourse to some of our examples of change, and perhaps we shall see how Aristotle's analysis of the causal structure of such changes accords very closely with our own common-sense view of the matter. We have already used as rough and ready examples the case of the young man who from having been unskilled is in process of learning a skill, or the case of the rubber band which from having been three inches long is in process of being stretched to six inches. Now requisite to both processes of change would be, in the first case, the fact that there is something that is able to be, and in the course of the change is actually in process of becoming, skilled; and, in the second case, the fact that there is something that is able to be, and that is actually in process of becoming, longer. In other words, in both cases it is just that something, or more exactly that material substance, which undergoes or sustains the change that is what Aristotle calls the material cause. Nor is it readily conceivable how, whether or not one chooses to call it a cause, there could possibly be any change at all without there being at least something or other that changes; and this is what Aristotle means by his material cause of change.

Somewhat comparable considerations apply as regards the formal cause. Since in the very nature of the case what any change involves is that that which undergoes the change—the matter or material cause—should eventually, and as a result of the process of change, acquire a new formal determination; that is to say, a mere potentiality of a thing to be thus and so must actually become thus and so as a result of the change. Consequently, what the thing thus becomes—the new form—is what Aristotle designates as being the formal cause of the change. For instance, in the case of the rubber band, since, through its being stretched, it actually becomes six inches long, it is just this new formal determination in respect to the rubber band's length or quantity that in such a case is said to be the formal cause of the change.

Note, though, that particular expression that was used in the last sentence about the rubber band's "being stretched." What exactly is it that accounts for this being stretched? Surely, in order for something to be in process of being stretched, there must be something that does the stretching. Nor does the mere fact that the band is able to be so stretched—the material cause—account for this actual stretching. And no less insufficient by way of accounting for this is the formal cause. That the band will eventually reach a length of six inches certainly does not suffice to explain its now being in process of being stretched or pulled to that length. Rather what is requisite in this connection is some actual force or power or agency that, as one might say, will do the stretching—or, in other words, that will do no less than actually produce or effect the change itself. It is this that Aristotle calls the *efficient cause* of the change; or, as he sometimes calls it, the agent of the change; or sometimes the moving cause, in the sense of the cause that is a mover, and this in the fully transitive sense of *to move*.

Here at last, then, we have a cause in a sense of the word that would be readily acceptable to us in English. For *cause* surely connotes for us something in the way of an actual efficacy or agency, which is hardly the thing suggested by Aristotle's material and formal cause. All the same, be it noted that no efficient cause could ever be thus effective in actually causing a change, unless that which was thus being changed were able to be changed (material cause), and unless also it were being changed to something—to some new form or formal determination, the formal cause. In this sense, then, an efficient cause or agent of the change is no more a sufficient condition of that change than are the material and formal causes. Rather all three are necessary conditions, and only jointly are they sufficient conditions of any change.

Nor, for that matter, are they in most instances even sufficient conditions of a change without the addition of still a fourth cause, or perhaps we had better say a fourth, but no less necessary, factor in change—what Aristotle calls the *final cause*. No sooner however, does one let that term slip out than it is as if a dirty word had been uttered. For Aristotelian final causes have been a favorite whipping boy of both scientists and philosophers since the seventeenth century, when Descartes started the fashion by venting his highly reputed scorn upon them.

But final causes are really neither so egregious nor so absurd as one might suppose. Of course, what has always been assumed to be so wrong with them is that since a final (from the Latin, *finis*) cause connotes an end or goal or purpose, to introduce final causes into nature and to suggest that such causes are among the necessary conditions even of the purely physical changes that take place in nature, is to conceive of such changes as if they were comparable to the purposive actions of human beings. And that is patently absurd: the wind doesn't blow, nor does water flow down hill, nor does fire burn, nor do physical bodies move, for a purpose. So enough of that!

Still, rather than being carried away by diatribes, let us look for a moment at the facts, so as to see not merely what Aristotle thought final causes are, but also how they function in an Aristotelian scheme of things. To this end, suppose we consider a few simple examples of natural or physical changes—say, of the sun shining on the stone sill of a window on a cold winter's day, or of a maple leaf changing from green to yellow in the autumn. In the former case as the rays of the sun strike the stone, the stone, from having been cool, becomes warm. Here, surely, is a simple, rudimentary instance of a change in quality: the stone (in this case, a substance and as such something that functions as the material cause of the change), from not being warm (privation) becomes warm (formal cause). Further, in this instance it is clearly the sun that is the efficient cause of the change: as one would say, it is the sun that actually warms the stone. Similarly, however difficult it may be for an amateur to specify exactly what they are, there is surely no doubt in the minds of any of us that there must be various agencies and influences (efficient causes) that act upon the leaf and so effect its change in color.

All the same, the moment we stop to reflect upon it, is it not obvious that the actions, influences, effects—call them what you will—of the various agencies and efficient causes that are operative in the natural world are always comparatively determinate, or, perhaps one should say, regular? Thus we expect the action of the sun's rays on the stone sill to have the effect of warming the sill, not of turning it blue, or of chipping it into a thousand pieces, or of standing it on end, or of causing it to fly off and float about like a cloud in the sky. Nor do the causes that act upon the leaf, so as to effect its change of color, ever turn it instead to stone, or magnify it to ten times its original size, or suddenly displace it to a different planet. In other words, since natural agents and efficient causes, as far as we can properly identify them and come to understand them, are found to have quite determinate and more or less predictable results, to that same extent we can also say that such forces and agencies are therefore ordered to their own appropriate consequences or achievements: it is these that they regularly tend to produce, and it is these that may thus be said to be their proper ends, though not, of course, in the sense of any deliberate or conscious purpose. Aristotelian final causes are no more than this: the regular and characteristic consequences or results that are correlated with the characteristic actions of the various agents and efficient causes that operate in the natural world.

Of course, if the agent or efficient cause from which a certain action proceeds should happen to be a human being, or, more precisely, an intelligent being, then clearly the final cause might well be the purpose, goal, and, in this sense, the end of that intelligent being who initiated the action. To return to our example of the rubber band, supposing that the effective force or agency causing the band to stretch was from a man's hand, then, clearly the purpose, and in this sense the final cause, of such action might well have been the person's desire to have the band extended to such length. So far as the young man who undertakes to learn a skill is concerned, it would presumably be his purpose that would be the final cause of his action. Yet for all of this, there is no reason at all why the final cause of an efficient action should necessarily be an end in the sense of a conscious purpose. On the contrary, as in anything that is being changed, the material cause that is undergoing the change is correlated with the formal cause, as being just that formal determination that the material potentiality is taking on or acquiring as a result of the change, so also the agent or efficient cause that effects the change is correlated with a final cause, which represents no more than the characteristic product or achievement that goes with that particular kind of efficient action.

Such, then, is the Aristotelian doctrine of the four causes. In fact, it amounts to very little more than an exfoliation and explication of our common-sense conviction that any change must be the change of something (material cause) from something (privation) to something else (formal cause), the change being necessarily effected by some agent (efficient cause) whose action may be presumed to be of a characteristic sort and productive of a characteristic result (final cause).

Again, the Plague of Modern Science and Modern Philosophy!

It may be all very well for us to say that quite obviously the Aristotelian account of change, with its three principles and its four causes, serves only to confirm and develop our own common-sense understanding of change and of the causes of change. At the same time, it is no less obvious that the entire testimony of both Aristotle and of common sense is decisively cancelled by no less than the entire history of modern science and modern philosophy, which hold that neither change nor the causes of change are at all what either Aristotle or common sense says they are.

Consider Galileo. His account of motion was directly at variance with Aristotle's. According to the Galilean view, as it was eventually summed up in one of Newton's so-called laws of motion: a body continues indefinitely in motion or at rest unless acted upon by an external force. In contrast, for Aristotle a body, far from continuing indefinitely in motion unless acted upon by external force, cannot even continue in motion in the first place unless acted upon by an external force.

Nor is there any secret about what led Galileo and the other great figures of seventeenth century science to break with Aristotle's account of motion. Put somewhat crudely and amateurishly, it was simply that in the motion of projectiles—for example, a cannon ball—the ball would appear to continue to move through the air with no readily discoverable efficient cause that could be said continuously to act upon the cannon ball and so to propel it. Yet on Aristotle's view such a continuing action of an efficient cause would be necessary if the body were to be kept moving at all.

Such is the issue. But what of its merits? A strange question, no doubt, since simply as a matter of history the failure of Aristotelian physics to explain projectile motion not only sounded the death knell of that physics, but resulted in so thorough and complete a burial that for three hundred years and more almost no one has thought the issue any longer worth discussing. Nor for our part will we attempt either to defend or rehabilitate any of the admittedly inadequate accounts of projectile motion supplied at various times by the Aristotelians. Rather let us content ourselves with considering some of the consequences of the now generally accepted modern view that continued motion stands in no need of a continuing efficient cause or mover.

At first blush the view is odd, to say the least, if not actually counter-intuitive. For if we consider not just motion alone (in Aristotle's sense, locomotion or change of place), but other sorts of changes as well (changes of quantity, say, or of quality), it would seem quite out of the question that anything should submit to a process of change without there being at least something that was changing it. Consider the rubber band again: is it possible that it could be in process of being stretched and stretched unless there was something actually doing the stretching? Or what about the sun's warming the stone: will the process of warming continue if the sun goes under a cloud and the rays no longer strike the stone sill at all? Or suppose that you stop blowing air into a balloon: does anyone imagine that the balloon will keep right on getting bigger and bigger, although air is no longer being forced into it?

Nor is it difficult to see why these things should be so, not just in fact, but in principle. If motion or change, in Aristotelian terms, is simply the actualizing of a potentiality, it is evident that potentialities don't actualize themselves. The tinder that I have gathered for a camp fire may well be inflammable, but it won't burn just of itself: something has to ignite it and the fire then to consume it. The stone sill may be potentially warm, but such a mere potentiality does not suffice for its actually becoming warm: something has to warm it.

Nor would even locomotion—at least when considered commonsensically—appear to be any exception to this rule. The book now lying on top of my desk can, of course, be moved to the bookshelf; or the tree that has blown across the road can be removed to a rather less inconvenient location; or my car which is in the garage can be moved around to the front of the house. Clearly none of these motions or removals can take place without something doing the moving: I must move the book; a bulldozer must move the tree; and the motor of the car has to be started, so that the car can be moved around to the front. Should I stop, or the bulldozer stop, or the motor stop, is it likely that the book will continue right on to the bookshelf, or the tree to the side of the road, or the car to the front of the house?

Moreover, granted that in other contexts and other reaches of our experience—say, for example, in the motion of projectiles—it does appear that things sometimes do continue in motion although there is nothing moving them, we can, of course, in order to take care of such cases, simply throw out Aristotle's conception of motion altogether and replace it with some variant on Newton's conception of inertial motion. Yet is inertial motion really intelligible, or is it not rather something that we merely posit as being so without understanding how or what it can be? For is not Aristotle right when he says that change or motion is nothing determinate: it is not a determinate quantity of anything or a quality or a relation or a place or a time or a position or what not? This is the very reason that Aristotle does not reckon motion to be among the categories. Instead, as he says, motion or change is an actualizing of a potency: it is an on-the-way from this to that without being either this or that. Nor is it conceivable how there can be such an actualizing of a potency without there being something that actualizes it; or how there can be anything that is in process of being changed (or altered or increased or decreased or what not) without there also being something that is changing it; or how there can be anything in motion without something moving it.

Very well, then, if we wish to insist that motion is really not this sort of thing at all, but rather is of the character of inertial motion, just how are we to understand the latter? We can no longer understand it as being the actualization of a potentiality, for that, as we have seen, entails that there be an efficient cause to actualize the potency. We might try perhaps, as did Descartes, simply to treat motion as a quality of the object moved. But that would be to instate change or motion as one of the categories—to treat it, in other words, as a definite form or determination of things. Yet surely our entire experience of change or motion runs against this, change being something that is not thus definite and determinate, but rather something that is a mere on-the-way, an in-process, a neither-this-nor-that. How, then, are we to understand so-called inertial motion? Apparently, there isn't any answer: we don't understand it; we just accept it, that's all.

Nor would it seem that one fares any better when, giving up on trying to understand motion or change in a non-Aristotelian sense, one follows the lead of modern scientists and philosophers in trying to understand the causal structure of change or motion. For if one may no longer think of change in terms of an efficient cause acting upon a material substance presumably for a certain finite period of time, so as to actualize a potentiality of that substance, the alternative would seem to be to think of an efficient cause as a mere event that happens before its effect and that, as it were, merely triggers that effect. For instance, to borrow a rather stock example from Hume, suppose that someone asks, "What caused the motion of the billiard ball across the table and into the pocket?" Answer: "The motion of the one ball was caused by the impact of another ball upon it." Clearly, though, the impact of the one ball upon the other preceded the motion of the second ball. From that, we can derive a fairly typical characterization in modern philosophy of the cause-effect relationship: "A cause precedes its effect."

How odd and embarrassing that is, however. For if a cause comes before its effect, how can a cause—in this case an efficient cause—act upon something so as to produce an effect? Thus, as Aristotle saw the matter, a cause never precedes its effect but rather the action of the cause is always concurrent and simultaneous with the production of the effect: as the knife is cutting the orange, the orange is being cut: as the rubber band is being stretched, something is stretching it; as the tree is being moved to the side of the road, the bulldozer is moving it. Substitute for this notion of causation the one of a cause as preceding its effect, and there is no way in which there can be either any causal action on anything or anything for the cause to act upon. Rather, when the effect comes into being, the cause will already have ceased to be. Hence there is no way in which an efficient cause can any longer be thought of as acting upon something so as actually to bring about its proper effect, with the result that the whole panoply of efficient, material, formal, and final causes simply goes out the window.

What, then, do we have in its place? The modern way is to conceive of a cause as simply an event, which in turn is followed by another event, the effect. But as to why the second event should follow upon the first has, since the time of Hume, been recognized as quite unintelligible. That *B* follows *A* may have been observed to occur repeatedly; but as to *why* *B* should follow *A,* and necessarily so, is something modern science and philosophy tell us is not understood and can never be. And little wonder, since the very machinery has been discarded by which the action of a cause as actually productive of its own effect could be understood.

Nor is this the only consequence of our modern habit of simply shrugging our shoulders when it comes to questions about the intelligibility of change in the modern sense, or of such cause-effect relations as are associated with change and motion in this sense. For if cause and effect are simply reduced to a schema in which event *B* is taken always to follow event *A,* it suddenly begins to appear that what we are left with is not in any proper sense our everyday world of change at all, but rather with a world of a quite unintelligible Zenonian succession of events.

But someone may say "For all of its philosophical unintelligibility, is not such a way of conceiving things extremely useful when it comes to the elaborate technological calculations necessary for that incredible control over nature which modern man has been so successful in achieving? Besides, have we not by now quite accustomed ourselves to looking at nature in this way, so that we no longer bother with the demands and requirements of our everyday, common-sense outlook?"

Perhaps, the answer to these questions may be, "Yes." Yet could it be that the price we pay for our uncritical accommodation to such a physics in the modern sense and all of its works is precisely that terrible schizophrenia of modern culture, which may well proceed from the fact that the world we have accommodated ourselves to philosophically and scientifically turns out to be a world that humanly and commonsensically we simply cannot live in?

Chapter III

Physics: The Nature of
Things Animate and Things Human

It may have seemed odd that the foregoing chapter should have presumed to be a presentation of Aristotle's "physics," so-called. For while it might be conceded that change or motion could be a proper concern of physicists, it would hardly seem to be their primary, and certainly not their only, concern. Nor would Aristotle himself be any less demanding than the rest of us in insisting that any study properly called *physics* would have to provide at least some account or picture of the physical universe as a whole—of the over-all frame of the heavens and the earth, of the seas, the sun, the moon, the stars. Besides, far from providing an account only of change or motion, Aristotle's *Physics* contains detailed and illuminating discussions of topics like time, infinity (both the infinite divisibility of things and the supposed infinite extent of the universe), chance, and even of the necessity of god's existence as a so-called prime mover with respect to various and sundry changes that go on in nature.

It being necessary, however, to condense as much as possible our present summary account of Aristotle's science and philosophy, we must content ourselves with saying only this much about

Aristotle's characteristic and distinctive picture of the physical universe as a whole: it is a picture of nature as seen from the perspective of the various kinds of change and motion that are appropriate to the different kinds of things or substances in the universe. Thus Aristotle felt that the heavens, so-called, were a series of concentric spheres to which the various heavenly bodies—sun, moon, planets, stars—were attached. Moreover, the proper motion of these spheres was eternally circular—of the sun around the earth, or of the moon, whose sphere was a different one from that of the sun, etc. But such details are only of historical interest.

Again, with respect to what might be called sublunary bodies and substances, Aristotle was no less empirical in his consideration than he was in his approach to the heavenly bodies. For as it seems obvious to our senses that the sun does move across the sky from east to west, so also it seems no less obvious to our senses that light bodies—for example, fire and air—tend to move upwards, and heavy bodies—for example, earth and water—tend to move downwards. Moreover, since, for various reasons we cannot now take time to consider, Aristotle was convinced that the earth was at the center of the universe and that the universe was finite in extent with certain outer limits or bounds, it was natural and proper that he should have considered it simply a fact confirmed by experience that light bodies like smoke or fire should rise upwards and move toward the periphery of the universe. On the other hand, heavy bodies like water and earth, as well as various compounds of them—wood, metals, our own bodies, etc.—if suspended in the air, should naturally fall to the ground, if their supports were removed.

But let us now move directly to a consideration of those things in nature which we call animate objects or living things. For as Aristotle felt that there was incontrovertible evidence of a characteristic kind of motion in the case of the heavens (namely, circular motion), as well as characteristic motions of the different elements (namely, either upward or downward motion), he also felt that living things undergo characteristic changes and developments that distinguish them alike from other sublunary substances like the four elements, as well as from the heavens.

Growth as the Motion or Change Characteristic of Living Things

What, for instance, about growth? All living beings or animate substances, Aristotle thought, are characterized by changes which may be called those of nutrition, growth, and reproduction. That these are changes in the proper sense there can be no doubt, for they manifest the three principles of change and are determined by the four causes of change. Yet even though the downward motion of a falling body or the circular motion of a heavenly body are no less changes and motions in their own right in that they exhibit the three principles and the four causes of change, we should not for a minute characterize them as being in any wise a growth or a development: a body in falling to the earth is not growing; nor is the sun said to be growing in its diurnal, circular movement around the earth.

What, then, is distinctive of growth, as being the sort of change or motion that is especially characteristic of living beings? To answer this question, it might be well to focus upon the peculiar way in which efficient causes are operative in such changes, as contrasted with the way they operate in regard to moving bodies in situations of the sort considered in the last chapter. In the latter case, as we saw, for a physical body to continue in motion (locomotion) it is obviously necessary that something continue to act upon it so as to move it; and presumably, the something that does the moving must be external to the thing moved. As it is expressed even in Newton's law, motion in one body—at least at its inception—is always a case of its being acted upon "by an external force."

In contrast, in the growth or development of a plant or an animal, there is a sense in which it could be said that absolutely no external force can ever make such a thing grow. Of course, it's true that without countless external factors like sunshine and rain, most plants could not grow or develop. But although these are necessary factors in the growth, let us say, of a maple tree, we would hardly say that the maple is pushed upward by these external factors or "causes"; instead, we recognize that, given the necessary conditions, the tree must grow simply of itself, or on its own. Nor is this to suggest that there is no moving cause or efficient cause, as Aristotle would call it, of the maple tree's growth, but rather that such a cause is not extrinsic or external to the plant thus made to grow, in quite the way in which a corresponding moving cause is from the outside and external to the physical body that it is said to move, or at least to set in motion.

Accordingly, expressed in Aristotle's terms, what this means is that in animate beings the efficient causes of such natural changes, motions, and developments as these beings are subject to are intrinsic to those beings themselves. Indeed, plants and animals might almost be said to have their own built-in "motors"—although, as we shall see presently, that could be a misleading way of putting the matter. Be that as it may, for the present we must take still another step if we are properly to incorporate all of these various common-sense considerations regarding the growth of plants and animals into Aristotle's over-all scheme. Interestingly, perhaps even oddly, Aristotle chooses to discuss all these phenomena of nutrition, growth, and even locomotion, in the case of plants and animals, under the heading of what is often referred to as his "psychology."

Aristotle's Definition of Soul or Psyche

Nor is the term *psychology,* considered etymologically, in any way inapt. Aristotle's own treatise on the subject is entitled Περι Ψυχησ; and this has customarily been translated with literal correctness as "On the Psyche or Soul." But *soul* is a word which in English has come to have all sorts of associations and connotations alien to Aristotle's understanding. It might better be rendered as simply the "psychic principle," or perhaps "animating principle," of living things. In fact, Aristotle in his time had no fewer difficulties with the Greek word ψύχη than we do with the word *soul,* when trying to understand what might presumably be intended in using such a term as supposedly appropriate to things that are alive. Almost invariably, both ψύχη in Greek and *soul* in English suggest a kind of separate entity or substance that is thought somehow to reside within a living body, to animate it and provide it with a kind of motor, and possibly even to survive it in an immortal life all of its own.

Such a way of conceiving of the soul or the psyche is seriously misleading in Aristotle's eyes. From his point of view, instead of thinking of the soul as being a special kind of substance or entity in its own right, it would be far more correct simply to regard the soul as being the "what" or the essential principle of a living thing. Surely, there is no denying that commonsensically we are impressed on every hand by manifest differences between things that are alive and things that are not, or between organic bodies and what we might call inorganic or mere physical bodies. In other words, a living thing is a different kind of substance from one that is inanimate or not alive: it will behave differently, will manifest different functions, and generally will simply be different from any and all inanimate substances. Accordingly, to say that a substance is animate or "besouled" is not to say that it houses a special piece of equipment called a soul or a spirit, but rather to say merely that it is the particular kind of substance that it is—a substance capable of performing certain life functions such as nutrition, growth, and reproduction, and possibly those of locomotion and sensation as well.

It is in this sense for Aristotle that a soul or psyche is only a certain kind of substantial form—a principle determining a living thing to be the kind of thing that it is. Moreover, as we have already seen, Aristotle insists that in the physical world heavy bodies are substances of a different kind from light bodies, and heavenly bodies of a still different kind from sublunary substances; and in each case the difference in kind is determined by the difference in its substantial form, form being defined by Aristotle as the principle of determinacy in things, in virtue of which each sort of thing is the kind of thing that it is and not some other kind. And so with respect to living things, what makes them the kinds of things they are as distinct from nonliving things, is simply their substantial form. To such substantial forms as are determinative of living things being the sort of things they are, Aristotle simply gives the name of *psyche* or *soul*.

No sooner, though, does one construe souls—plant souls, animal souls, human souls—as being simply so many substantial forms through which these various kinds of living things become or are determinately the kinds of things they are, then one must also remember that forms are usually correlative with matter. That something should be determinately this or that would presumably require not only a form as a principle of such determinateness, but also matter as being that which is thus rendered determinate through the reception of a form. Or to use one of Aristotle's own illustrations, for there to be an imprint of the seal in the wax it is requisite not only that there be the form of the imprint, but also that there be the wax to receive the determinate imprint; form is to matter, as the imprint in the wax is to the wax.

Further, since it is living things—plants, animals, human beings—that we are presently concerned with, it is obvious as we have already remarked that all of them are subject to various kinds of changes, especially the developmental changes characteristic of living beings. In any case, from the foregoing chapter it will be recalled that for anything to undergo a change of whatever kind, it is requisite that matter be recognized as one of the indispensable principles of such change. Accordingly, what all of these considerations point to is that if for Aristotle the soul or psyche is to be regarded as no more and no less than that formal principle of determinacy, in virtue of which living things are the kinds of things they are, then such a formal principle requires a material principle as its correlative: there must be something that is thus made determinate, or that takes on its specific character, through the reception of a form—namely, matter. What's more, if a living being or animate being is to change or develop at all, there must be within it that which makes it able to change, a certain principle of potentiality, something that is not either this or that, but is only potentially this or that, namely, matter.

In living beings, moreover, the material principle that is thus correlative with the soul or form is simply the body. For example, in animals is it not the animal's body which may be said to be a living body? So likewise for plants and for men. In all such cases the soul is to the body as form to matter. Of course, it is not just any kind of physical body—any old "stock or stone or senseless thing"—that is capable of being a living body. Only such a body as Aristotle called an organic body is susceptible of life or may be said to be potentially alive. So it is that Aristotle's definition of the soul is that a soul is a substantial form, the "what-it-is" of a certain kind of thing; moreover, that of which the soul is thus the "what" or the substantial form can only be a body, a physical body; and yet a physical body of a distinctive sort, one that can function as a living body or, as Aristotle calls it, an organic body, a body that is potentially alive.

This must not be interpreted to mean that an organic body exists first, and only afterwards receives its soul or substantial form, thereby coming to be actually alive for the first time. That would be to degrade the soul from being a substantial form to being a mere accidental form. As should already have become clear from the discussion of the preceding chapter, in any accidental change, that which underlies or sustains the change is always a substance. Thus a man from being in one place can move to another, or from being small can become large, or from being ignorant can become informed. But in undergoing such changes, the man does not cease to be a man; instead, all such changes are to be reckoned as mere changes in the accidents of a substance, as contrasted with a change of that substance itself into an entirely different substance. Accordingly, if one and the same physical body were to undergo a change from not being alive to being alive, that would be only an accidental, not a substantial, change. Surely, though, Aristotle is right in insisting that a living being is necessarily a substance in its own right, and as such possessed of a substantial form different from that of any inanimate substance. Similarly, if one is ever to speak of anything as coming alive, it must not be supposed that this is a case of one and the same physical body or substance being now without life and then later coming to have life; for this would be no more than an accidental change of one and the self-same substance. Instead, for anything to come alive would involve actual substantial change, in which a new substance would come into being. And underlying any such substantial change could only be what Aristotle called *prime matter;* that is to say, it could not be any already informed matter as in the case of an actual physical body, for then the change would be only accidental. Rather that which receives or becomes determined by a substantial form must be prime matter, or matter which in itself is completely undetermined, being no more than a capacity or potentiality to become determinate, or to become something.

It is in the light of such considerations that Aristotle defines, still more precisely, the soul or psyche as being that which brings about a primary or initial actualization of something that is alive or, if you will, of a living body able to perform such life functions as nutrition, growth, and reproduction. Once such a thing as a living substance has thus come into being, all of such subsequent actions represent changes in a substance that is already existing; as such they are in the proper sense of the term *accidental changes* which the existing substance undergoes.

As a result of sustaining these further and subsequent changes, that substance comes to acquire still new and further determinations: for instance, it probably comes to be larger than it was, perhaps of a different color, maybe even located in a different place, and certainly possessed of any number of features and characteristics which it did not have at its original inception or coming into being. All of these are only so many new and subsequent accidental forms of that same substance. Since these forms are only the actualization of various potentialities of that substance, they are sometimes spoken of as second acts or second actualizations of that substance, as contrasted with the initial or primary actualization of the substance itself.

In other words, the soul or psyche is just that primary actualization as a result of which a living substance comes into being; or, put a little differently, the soul or psyche is no less than the substantial form that makes a living thing to be and to be the kind of thing it is. And so we find Aristotle employing two rather striking figures to bring out this characteristic relation of the soul to the body. Suppose, he says, that an ordinary tool such as an axe were no mere artifact but a natural body in its own right: then the very whatness or quiddity of the axe—that is, its specific cutting quality—would be, as it were, the soul or substantial form of the axe.[1] Or again, he says, suppose that an eye, instead of being a mere organ of the body, were itself no less than a living animal: then the sight of the eye would be its soul or substantial form.[2]

When the soul is understood in this way as being the very whatness or quiddity or substantial form of the body—as that which makes a living thing to be just that, alive or living—then there is no longer a problem as to whether or how the soul and the body can be one. As Aristotle remarks, it is no more difficult to understand how the body and the soul can be one, than it is to understand how the wax and the imprint on the wax are one. Thus as no one mistakes the imprint of the wax for a separate substance existing apart from the wax, so likewise one ought never to mistake the soul or psyche for a separate substance existing apart from the living body, the latter being simply the matter which the soul animates or renders determinate as an actual living body.

The Soul as Cause

No sooner, though, does one understand the soul thus as being a form, which stands to the organic body which it animates or be-souls simply as form to matter, than it immediately becomes possible better to understand the soul in what might be called its causal role. If the soul is precisely the substantial form of a living body or substance, then on Aristotle's notion of causes as being four-fold—formal, material, efficient, and final—the soul will certainly be the formal cause of that of which it is the substantial form. In fact, a substantial form, as we have already noted, is simply that which determines a thing to be what it is, or to be a thing of the kind that it is, and not some other kind. However, no sooner does anything, no matter what, come to have a determinate nature of any kind, than certain consequences must follow. To fall back on a somewhat crude and obvious illustration, if something is a triangle, then necessarily it will have an angle sum equal to two right angles. But so also, if something is a living thing, then necessarily those features and characteristics that are proper to living things as contrasted with nonliving things will come to pertain to it. In fact, earlier in this chapter, we had occasion to call attention to the fact that living beings or living substances manifest a characteristic kind of change or motion—what we called for want of a better term *developmental change*.

Suppose, then, that we ask somewhat gratuitously, "But how does it happen that living things should thus move or change in this characteristic way?" Is not the answer simply that they do so merely because they are the kind of things they are, that it pertains just to the nature of an animate being or living being to move or behave in a way that is characteristic of such beings, much as it simply pertains to the nature of a triangle to have an angle sum of two right angles? Nor does this amount to anything other than what Aristotle would understand by a formal causation; that is to say, the soul as the substantial form of a living substance determines—or, as an Aristotelian might say, formally causes—that substance to be the kind of substance that it is, and thus to display the characteristic features and properties that pertain to things of that kind as contrasted with things of other kinds.

As soon as it is established that the soul is a formal cause in the sense just indicated, curiously enough it seems to follow that the soul must be an efficient or moving cause as well. For one thing, our foregoing discussion would certainly seem to indicate that the soul as the substantial form of a living substance presumably must formally cause or determine such a substance to just that type of developmental change that is appropriate to things animate. Not only that, but we have also noted it to be a feature of such developmental change that no external force can ever make a thing or substance change in this way. Nothing can make a plant grow; rather, as we might say, that is something the plant has to do itself. True, there are all sorts of things that can be done to aid that growth or to facilitate it; but in the final analysis, a plant has to do its own growing and that's that!

To say this, however, is to say that the moving cause of the actual growth of a plant must be intrinsic to the plant. And what else could such a moving cause be other than the soul or the substantial form itself? We have already seen how for Aristotle, no less than for common sense, it is necessary that in any ongoing process of change—for example, in growth or in locomotion—as the change is being effected, there must be something that is effecting the change. Besides, the way in which Aristotle conceives of what might be called the actual efficiency of an efficient or moving cause is as an action of an agent upon a material substratum or patient, which, insofar as it is thus acted upon, is thereby in process of being changed. Accordingly, in the case of a plant that is growing, or of an animal or a man that is moving from one place to another, it is the body, or at least certain parts of the organic body, that are being acted upon.

Moreover, it is important to remember that in Aristotle's understanding of change, the change that is being effected is always and as such in the patient, and not in the agent of the change: that is to say, the agent of a change is not itself changed in the process, unless accidentally; rather it is properly only the patient that suffers the change. Of course, this may strike us as being puzzling at first, so accustomed are we to thinking of motion or change in terms of one billiard ball (the agent) moving across the table and striking a second billiard ball (the patient). And indeed in such a case not only is the agent of the change itself in motion at the time of the change, but also the one ball in striking the second undergoes a reaction in its impact on the first. But all this is largely accidental to the situation that prevails in regard to moving bodies. More generally, and considered as such, for an agent to act upon a patient so as to change it means, quite precisely, that it is the patient that is changed, and not the agent, unless it be only accidentally.

Applying this analysis then to the soul, insofar as it is active as the moving cause of changes in the body, it follows that those changes are changes in the body, but not in the soul. Nor is it necessary to confound the picture by trying to imagine the soul as being in its own right a moving cause after the fashion of a billiard ball, and which therefore effects changes in the body only by a physical impact upon it. This obviously is to introduce a confusion worse confounded, and one which is neither necessary nor relevant to understanding the action of the soul as a moving cause upon the body, and thus as being effective of various changes that go on in the body, the latter being simply the very patient that undergoes the changes.

Apparently, then, the soul is to be understood as functioning no less as a moving cause than as a formal cause. Nor may we stop there, for the soul is equally a final cause as well. As we have already been at pains to explain, any efficient cause is to be understood as having a certain determinate kind of effect, which in the somewhat misleading but still accurate, old-fashioned terminology of final causes would be expressed by saying that any efficient cause acts for a certain end. Very well, are not those developmental changes that take place in living things—nutrition, growth, locomotion, sensory perception, etc.—are these not all changes directed to what might be called the full life or full flowering of the plant or animal in question? That is to say, these changes are both conducive to and bear out what it is to be a living thing of that specific kind. But what-it-is-to-be a plant or an animal or a man is nothing more nor less than the substantial form of that plant or animal or man. Hence the soul or psyche as the substantial form of a living being serves no less as the final cause than as the moving cause of the various characteristic changes that living or animate bodies undergo. And so the entire doctrine of the causal role of the soul is summed up by Aristotle in the words:

> The soul is the cause or source of the living body. The terms cause and source have many senses. But the soul is the cause of its body in all three senses which we explicitly recognize. It is (a) the source or origin of movement, it is (b) the end, it is (c) the substance [in the sense of substantial form] of the whole living body.[3]

A Possible Complication

Unfortunately, the foregoing account of the causal role of the soul in the life of things animate is scarcely completed than it must be acknowledged to give rise to a certain complication. The complication has directly to do with that general account of the causes of change given in the preceding chapter. It will be remembered that the key example of change there put forward as requiring Aristotle's typical four-fold causal analysis was the example of physical change in the ordinary sense—that is, the sort of change in which a physical body is moved locally as a result of an external force being applied to it. In contrast, the changes which in this chapter we have suggested as characteristic of living things are what we have loosely termed developmental changes. In their case, the efficient or moving cause, we argued, was not to be thought of as an external force coming from the outside, but rather as a force intrinsic to the living substance (be it plant, animal, or human being) that was subject to such changes or motions. Accordingly, it was just on this basis that we sought to distinguish the sorts of changes and motions that are characteristic of the biological realm (that is, the realm in which the soul as a principle intrinsic to living beings is at the same time the efficient cause of the movements and changes of these beings) from changes that are characteristic of the physical universe (that is, the universe in which physical substances are subject to motions and changes produced by efficient causes that are external to those substances).

Nevertheless, this particular way of contrasting the physical with the biological, or perhaps better, the inanimate with the animate, is not really the way in which Aristotle himself would point the contrast. The contrast is not totally alien to the spirit of Aristotle's over-all account of the various changes in nature and of their four-fold causal structure. Still, it does differ from that account in one not insignificant respect; and for reasons of historical accuracy, if not of philosophical import, that difference ought at least to be mentioned.

Already we have had occasion to note in passing that in Aristotle's eyes the motion characteristic of the heavenly spheres is an eternal circular motion; and for sublunary bodies, the motion characteristic of so-called heavy bodies is a downward motion toward the center of the universe, and of light bodies an upward motion toward the periphery of the universe. In all of these cases, though, it is not Aristotle's view that the efficient cause of the motion is an external force—at least not in the sense in which the pushing of a cart up a hill requires a continuous application of an external force on the cart. In fact, one might almost say that, considering the four elements (earth, air, fire, and water) and the physical bodies that are compounded out of them, Aristotle tends to approximate his account of the motions of such bodies much more to his account of the motions of animate bodies than he does to his account of the motions of bodies acted upon by external forces.

True, he does not go so far as to say that earth and water, for example, have souls which cause such bodies to move downwards, or air and fire souls that cause them to move upwards. On the other hand, he does distinguish between the natural motion of such bodies and what might be called their counter-natural or violent motion. Thus, for example, a heavy body, if it is forcibly moved upwards, is being subjected to a counter-natural or violent motion; on the other hand, its downward motion toward the center of the universe is natural.

What, then, may be said to be the moving causes of such respective motions, natural and violent? Well, of a violent or counter-natural motion, such as that of a heavy body being moved upward, the moving cause must be an external force applied continuously from the outside to the body that is in process of being moved. Indeed, the sort of motion which in the preceding chapter we put forward as being an example of the typical sort of motion of bodies in the physical world now turns out to be, in Aristotle's eyes, not an example of the natural motion of such bodies, but rather of their counter-natural or violent motion.

On the other hand, what of their natural motion? What is the moving cause in the case of such a natural motion—for example, of the natural motion of a heavy body downward? Unhappily, to this question Aristotle's answer is somewhat vacillating and unsure.[4] First, he suggests that if a heavy body is being suspended in the air and thus prevented from falling naturally to the ground, all that is needed is that the supports be removed and the body will then fall naturally to the ground. Hence it might occur to someone to maintain that the causes of the supports' being removed are the causes of the body's falling.

Yet this account Aristotle himself finds not altogether satisfactory. Obviously, the cause of a support's being removed is only, as it were, indirectly and accidentally a cause of the body's falling. What, though, as such is the direct and proper cause of the downward motion? It cannot be that such bodies are moved by a force from within themselves, for that would invest them with a soul as a sort of built-in moving cause or intrinsic principle of change, which is appropriate only to living beings and not to inanimate beings. Instead, Aristotle suggests, physical bodies like earth, air, fire, and water, and their compounds, must be regarded as having a certain power of motion by their very nature. Hence if there is nothing to impede the exercise of such a power, a heavy body will naturally move downwards. Moreover, if one persists in wanting to know what the precise agent or moving cause of that motion is as such, Aristotle's answer is that the agent of the motion can only be identified with the efficient cause that brought a body of such and such a nature, and with that its power of motion, into being in the first place.

Alas, there is no denying that this account of the natural motions of physical bodies is far from satisfactory. Still, a consideration of motion of this kind, in contrast to the violent motions of those same physical bodies, and in contrast again to the natural motions of organic or living bodies, should give one a sense of Aristotle's over-all appreciation of the nature and variety of changes that go on in the world of nature, as well as of the causes of those changes.

The Status of Man
in the Hierarchy of Nature

What has become, though, of the promise held out in the title of this chapter to discuss not only things animate, but things human? It goes without saying that, even on a common-sense basis, a human being is a living or animate being. Hence any discussion of those motions and changes that are characteristic of living things will apply to human beings as well. After all, human beings do grow, they do digest food, they do reproduce themselves, etc. But, then, human beings are not merely living beings either; they are physical bodies as well. In consequence, as physical bodies, human beings are subject to the various natural and violent motions that pertain to the four elements and their compounds.

Nor does Aristotle neglect common-sense considerations of this kind in determining what might be called the sort of cumulative hierarchy of substances that are extant in the natural world. Indeed, Aristotle's doctrine might be set forth crudely in the following fashion. In the hierarchy of nature, plants are ranked above mere physical bodies. But to say that plants are thus "above" physical bodies means no more than that plants themselves are, of course, physical bodies, and that all of the laws of motion and change that apply to physical bodies apply also to plants; but at the same time, plants, in addition to obeying the laws of motion of physical bodies, also manifest a type of change or motion of their own—what we have called developmental change—which mere physical bodies as inanimate things do not manifest at all.

Similarly, moving to the next stage in the hierarchy, animals are above plants in that, in addition to performing the ordinary vital functions associated with mere plant life, animals also perform the further—and in this sense the "higher" and more complicated—

functions of sensation and locomotion. With respect to this latter point, Aristotle obviously felt that animals are capable of moving about from place to place under their own power, whereas plants are not.

Finally, as regards human beings, they, of course, perform all of the lower vital functions—nutrition, growth, and reproduction, and on top of these sensation and locomotion—but, in addition, they are capable of a still higher cognitive operation than those of mere sensation, namely, of rational cognition and understanding. Recalling our discussions of the preceding sections, in the case of each of these living substances—plants, animals, and men—it is the soul which determines each kind of substance to the performance of the functions or changes appropriate to substances of that kind with the result that it is the formal, final, and efficient causes of those characteristic functions and changes. Thus, to consider human beings simply as substances in the natural world is to consider the human soul as being determinative of the various human functions that human beings perform. What's more, since the distinctive function of men lies in the exercise of rational knowledge and understanding, it is naturally this function that one needs to concentrate upon in any study of man as man.

Rational Cognition As Distinctive of Human Beings: Some Preliminaries

Since for Aristotle rational cognition in men presupposes and depends radically upon the more fundamental animal function of sensory cognition, it is necessary to examine this first. By way of further orientation, it should be remarked perhaps that thus far, both in this chapter and in the preceding one, we have considered the various kinds of natural substances through the characteristic motions or changes that they undergo. It is from a similar perspective that we might perhaps approach the study of human beings or human nature. Yet for Aristotle actual knowing, as well as actual sensing, are not properly changes or motions at all. Rather they are what Aristotle would call activities, which come about as a result of certain changes having taken place, but which themselves are properly classifiable under the categories as determinate ways of being, as contrasted with mere ways of becoming. Accordingly, remaining true to the orientation which we have observed so far, we shall consider human beings not so much with respect to their activities of knowing, but rather with respect to the processes involved in their coming to know.

At the outset, too, it should be noted that when Aristotle turns his attention to the processes of sensory cognition in animals and of rational cognition in men, he does so on the presupposition of a thorough-going philosophical realism. Such a realism may be briefly summed up in two dominant considerations: (1) the consideration that the things of the world simply are what they are in themselves and independently of our attitudes toward them or our opinions about them; and (2) the consideration that human beings are capable—subject, of course, to all sorts of errors and mistakes that they may commit in the process—of coming to know such things of the world more or less adequately, but nonetheless as they are in themselves and not merely as we take them to be.

The last point perhaps deserves reiteration, it being so much the accepted fashion in philosophy nowadays to suppose that whatever may be the character of things in themselves (and whether they may even have any character at all in themselves), it is not as such that we come to know them, but only as they appear to us and as we take them to be. Contemporary philosophers and people generally, that is, today tend to assume that the mechanisms through which we perceive things and the categories in which we understand them constitute, as it were, a sort of distorting medium, through which and only through which things can come to be known to us. As a result, the current common assumption is that we never come to know things as they are in themselves, but only as they appear as or present themselves to us through the distorting medium of our various cognitive faculties and devices.

Not so for Aristotle! For him the entire enterprise of studying human cognition and the operations of our cognitive faculties is one of trying to see just how the mechanisms of these operations, as well as the instruments and devices that we employ in these operations, are thoroughly adapted, not to distorting things, but rather to disclosing or representing them just as they are.

Sensory Cognition As a Presupposition of Rational Cognition

What about sensory cognition, then, as Aristotle understands it? Well, it is hardly surprising that he should say that there are five senses—sight, hearing, taste, touch, and smell. This surely is no more than common sense, and many would say perhaps that it is no better than an uncritical or stone-age common sense as well. But Aristotle would go on to insist still further—and again common-sensically—that there are, corresponding to each of the five senses, certain qualities in physical objects, the various ones of which qualities each of the different senses is peculiarly adapted to apprehending. Now these qualities in physical objects are called *the proper sensibles,* precisely in that each of the different qualities is proper to one of the sensory faculties—colors are proper to sight, sounds to hearing, flavors to taste, odors to smell, and qualities like hard and soft, rough and smooth etc. to touch.

Clearly, though, such qualities are seldom if ever presented to us in isolation. Rather the colors that we see are invariably colors on surfaces which are of various sizes and shapes. Or the sound that we hear may be coming from one place, or it may be moving. Again, what we feel as we put out our hands may be one thing, or it may be several. What about these further qualities of objects, over and above their colors, sounds, odors, tactile qualities etc.? Aristotle enumerates them as being those of shape, size, number, motion and rest, etc. And he designates them as *common sensibles* rather than proper sensibles, for the reason that such qualities, instead of being the proper objects of but one sense, are common to the several different senses. For is not one able to feel as well as see the shape of an object, or perhaps hear an object in motion, as well as see or feel it to be so?

Now for still another step in this enumeration of what it is that we sense in our acts of sensory cognition. For is it the case that when we see something, what we see is no more, say, than just a patch of color of a certain size and shape; or when we hear something, is it never any more than just a sound, be it far or near, or perhaps moving or in place? Is it not rather the case that seeing usually, if not always, is more than seeing just colored shapes of various sizes? It is seeing the color of an automobile, or the shape of a man, or what not. Likewise, hearing is usually more than just hearing a sound. Instead, we hear the sound of horn or of a voice or of thunder, etc. In other words, sensing would certainly seem to be more than simply apprehending the proper and the common sensibles; in addition it is also an affair of apprehending the things or the objects or, as Aristotle would say, the substances that have those various qualities of color, sound, shape, position, etc.

For that matter, referring to our earlier discussion of Aristotle's categories, it will be remembered that we put it forward as being at once obvious and undeniable that such a thing as color or size, for example, simply could not be or exist save as the color or size of something. Nor could there be a noise without its being the noise of something, or a motion without its being the motion of something, etc. So now when we make the transition from a consideration of what is requisite for things to be or to exist, to a consideration of what is requisite for their coming to be known, we find that sensory cognition or awareness involves an awareness not just of proper and common sensibles, but also of the things or substances in which such qualities must necessarily be or exist. At the same time, it is clear that the thing that is colored is not a proper object of the sense of sight in the way that the color itself is; nor is a substance directly sensed in quite the way that a common sensible like size or shape is sensed. Instead, it is as if the substances which sustain or are characterized by the various qualities from among the proper and common sensibles are sensed only indirectly; or, as Aristotle would put it, such things are sensed only accidentally, or are objects of sense only *per accidens.*

Little wonder, too, that, with respect to these indirect objects, or objects *per accidens,* of our senses, our sensory awareness is peculiarly subject to error. The plane that I think I see in the sky turns out to be only a bird; or the noise that I hear in the street below proves not to be from the traffic but from the excavation for a new sewer line.

Requisite Features of Cognition, Both Sensory and Intellectual

For the present, though, let this suffice by way of an account of the sorts of objects that we may be said to perceive through our senses. What, though, of the actual process or mechanism of such sensing? What is it that goes on in the process of sensation, such that, say, the color red from being merely a quality of an object in the world comes to be a quality that is known or apprehended? How, in other words, is the change or transformation brought about from something's merely being to its being known? In answer to this question one might say that Aristotle does indeed, in a somewhat odd sense of the word perhaps, understand this process to be a kind of trans*form*ation or, better perhaps, a kind of communication of *forms*. For Aristotle would consider the key to knowledge of any kind, be it sensory or intellectual knowledge, to lie precisely in what he calls forms. We have already seen how it is through forms—in Aristotle's technical sense of that term—that anything and everything in the world is what it is, or is the kind of thing that it is. Now, similarly, Aristotle is going to say that it is through their forms, and only through them, that things in the world can come to be known. Nor is it difficult to see why this should be so. For if a thing is what it is only in virtue of its form or forms, then clearly if anything is ever to be known for what it is, that must also presumably be through its form or forms. So it is, as we suggested, that for Aristotle the process of knowledge must be understood as involving a literal transformation of sorts—a transformation of a form from being that in virtue of which a thing is what it is to being that in virtue of which that thing comes to be known for what it is.

Before we come to any specific consideration of the mechanism of sensory cognition as over against that of intellectual cognition, and vice versa, let us first attempt to see if certain requisite features of this transformation may not be determined just in general and in the abstract. As a first requisite, may we not say that if it is through their forms that the forms or determinate natures of things come to be known, then such forms must somehow be communicated to and received in the knower, in order that through them the forms of things in reality may come to be known? Second, if forms are received in the soul (and more specifically, as we shall see presently, this means either in the sensory faculties or in the intellect), in order that through them the forms in things may come to be known, then somehow the forms in the soul must be capable of being identified with the forms in things. After all, given Aristotle's realism, to take a simple example, if I am to know the red color of an object, it must indeed be that identical color that I come to know, and not something other than it or even very like it. But consider that if I know something only very like X but not X itself, then I do not know X. Yet the requirements of a realism are that I must be able to know things (and hence X as one among them) just as they are in themselves.

Given these two prime requisites of all knowing, how is it that, in order to fulfill the first requisite, forms may be understood to be communicated from things to the soul? Responding to this challenge, Aristotle considers that what is here being called for is an explanation of a certain kind of change, and more specifically of a change from a form's not being in the soul to its being in the soul. Further in the explanation of any change, Aristotle reckons that the four causes have to be brought into play. Thus if it is the red color of the object that has to be taken up and apprehended and received into the soul, then the formal cause of such change is that quality of red which from first being in the object comes to be in the soul (or more specifically in this case in the sensory faculty). As for the material cause, it can be no other than just that potentiality of the soul, or of the particular cognitive faculty of the soul, to receive the form. Then, of course, there must be some agent of this change, and, needless to say, the agent aims at achieving the aforementioned end, which is simply the actualizing of the form in the soul.

Unfortunately, no sooner is the process of coming to know described in this way than it would seem to be reduced to a mere ordinary change in the natural world. And this it cannot properly be at all. Suppose that instead of our talking about the form or quality of red being received cognitively in the soul, we were to talk instead of the wood of a fence receiving a red color from a paint brush. Clearly, in the latter case no less than in the former, one could spell out the four causes of the change; and yet the patent difference between the two cases would be unmistakable: when the fence becomes red from having been painted, we do not say that it therefore knows the color red, but rather that it is red; on the other hand, when a cognitive faculty of the soul receives a form—in this case the color red—we do not say that the soul itself thereby becomes red, but rather that it comes to know the red color.

Moreover, this difference between what might be called an ordinary physical change in an object and a cognitive change in a knower, Aristotle would account for by what might well be considered a somewhat *ad hoc* distinction. In effect, he says that what we have called the cognitive reception of a form in the soul is not a reception of form in matter at all. True, the soul does receive forms, and as such it stands to the forms which it receives as potency to act; and for this reason it can even loosely be said to play the role of material cause in the process of coming to know. Yet for all this, the reception of forms in the soul is an immaterial and not a material reception. Moreover, what marks the distinction between the two sorts of receptions is something that we have already touched upon. Thus when a form is materially received, the recipient itself becomes determinate precisely in the mode of that very form: the fence in being painted red receives the form red and thus actually becomes a red fence; the stone from being cool actually becomes warm itself; the billiard ball from having been in one place actually comes to be in a new and different place. In contrast, when a form is immaterially received, as in the soul, the soul does not thereby take on the character of that form, but rather through that form comes to know that very same form in reality. Thus in receiving the form of red, my sight does not become red, but rather I see the color red through that same form. Or again, in apprehending, and so in receiving into the soul, the substantial form of a tree, or the what-it-is-to-be a tree, I do not thereby become a tree, but rather I come to know a tree.

Further, it is this notion of an immaterial reception of forms in the soul that is Aristotle's resource for meeting the second requisite feature of any realistic theory of knowledge. That feature, it will be remembered, is that of the form that is received in the soul having to be identical with that same form as it exists in the thing known. Otherwise, we should never be able to know things in the world as being those very things that they are. However, if a form—say that of the red color of some object—is received immaterially in the soul, then that form will have been both abstracted and separated from the material conditions under which it happens to exist in the thing known. Moreover, the reception of the form by the knower being an immaterial reception, the form itself cannot be said to have been subjected to any new and different material conditions in the soul. Instead, it will be only that very form as such, which can be none other than the same identical form, be it in the soul, or in the object, or wherever. In fact, if we ask what it is that distinguishes the color red in its different instances or manifestations, it is the fact that this color is received into, and becomes a quality of, quite different material objects—red pencils, red skies, red fences, red faces, red leaves, etc. But once the color red is freed from such material and individuating conditions, as is done in the process of cognition, then perforce the red which I apprehend in my sensory or intellectual faculties will be the same identical red that is in the object. That is why it is this very immaterial reception of forms in the soul that is the decisive factor that makes knowledge possible—it makes possible our being able to know, through an immaterially received form in the sense or in the intellect, that very same form as it exists in the object, and through which that object is what it is.

The Specifics of Sensation and Intellection

Given these requisites of cognition, how, more specifically, may sensory cognition, and then again intellectual cognition, be seen to meet such requisites? As regards sensory cognition, it should perhaps be apparent already from our discussion of the external senses that the sphere or domain of such cognition is strictly limited. Be it sight, touch, hearing, smell, or taste, what it is that the process of cognition in such cases culminates in is never more than the apprehension of certain specific qualities: colors, sounds, odors, and the like. It is simply a matter of common sense that such qualities cannot be apprehended unless they are, as we might say, physically transmitted to the various sense organs. We don't hear sounds unless they strike upon our eardrums; we only taste things that are on the tongue; and even sight requires that colors be conveyed to the eye. Still, the mere contact with or presence in the sense organ of a sensory quality does not suffice for that quality actually to be sensed. The organ is quite literally no more than an *organ* or instrument of sensation, and it is the sense faculty or sensory power that actually uses the organ. Or put a little differently, the organ must actually be functioning as an organ of sensation if there is to be any actual sensing. Hence the mere presence of a flavor on the tongue does not suffice for that flavor actually to be sensed, especially if the taste buds have been injured or impaired, so that the organ cannot function.

What is it that happens when the organ does function properly? We have already seen that one of the things that is requisite for any sort of knowledge or cognition is that that which comes to be known must be present in the knower in some way other than by a mere physical or material presence. Thus, however much the flavor may be physically present on the tongue, it is necessary before it can actually be sensed that it be in some sense immaterially or intentionally[5] present to the sense faculty. The way Aristotle expresses this is to say that the sensory faculty receives only the form of that which is sensed, but without the matter. What he means by this, presumably, is that in seeing a color, our eyesight, for example, does not itself become colored, in the manner of a material recipient taking on a new form; rather what the sight receives is just the form, say, of the particular red color that has been transmitted to the eye, so that although the pupil of the eye may indeed have become red on at least a part of its surface, the eyesight itself is not red. Moreover, once the form of red—or of a sweet taste on my tongue, or of a Middle-C sound in my ear, or of a certain odor in my nostrils—is received without matter, then the second of those requisite features of cognition will thereby also be found to have been met, that there must be an actual identity of my apprehension of a form and the form that is apprehended. That is what Aristotle means when he suggests that for a sense faculty such as that of hearing actually to be hearing is the same as for a sound actually to be sounding.[6] That is to say, the two actualities of the sense faculty and of the sound are one and the same, even though considered simply as potentialities a sense faculty that is capable of hearing is a very different sort of thing from an ordinary physical object that has, say, a capacity for emitting a sound.

Now, partly by way of contrast, consider intellectual cognition. Once again, as in sensory cognition so also in intellectual cognition, it is through forms in the soul that the forms of things—those forms in virtue of which things are what they are and have the determinate characteristics that they do have—come to be known.

How, though, do these forms get into the intellect in the case of intellectual cognition?

In answering this question, one must begin by noting certain fairly obvious and generally recognized differences between knowledge as purveyed by the senses and that which comes through the intellect. Take, for example, the color red. As a form that is the source of that determinate feature that is present in any and all red objects, the redness of any particular red object can be perceived by the senses only when the red color is actually present to the eyes. That is to say, I cannot properly be said to see the color red unless that color is actually before my eyes. Also any red that I see must always be a particular red or, better, that particular red that is being conveyed to my eyes right here and now.

Not so, however, with intellectual cognition. It is, for example, perfectly possible to think about the color red or to have a concept of redness without any red object being visually present to my senses. Not only that, but any concept or idea which I have of red is necessarily a concept that is applicable to any and every red object. A red tie, a red leaf, a red book, a red sunset are all of them equally red: one and the same concept applies to them all. Or to use the standard philosophical term, it is simply that any concept or idea of red is perforce universal; or, in more Aristotelian terms, such a concept is a concept of the form red, whatever may be the substances that that form happens to be present in, and wherever and whenever it may be so present in them.

Accordingly, given these characteristics of intellectual cognition as over against sensory cognition, Aristotle insists that the former is obviously not dependent upon any physical or bodily organ as is the latter. Indeed, it is precisely because sounds must strike the ear, or colors be conveyed to the eye, or flavors be on the tongue, that the perception by the senses of these qualities must always be a perception of those particular qualities that are present to the senses right here and now. The red that I see is just this particular red that is present to my eyes now. In contrast, since the notion or concept that I have of red is universal, and hence is not tied down to any particular red that is currently present to the senses, it would seem to follow that the intellect in its apprehension of forms is not tied down to any particular receptor organ, as is the faculty of sense.

Likewise, the intellect in its apprehension and knowledge of objects is not restricted to any mere apprehension or awareness of sensory qualities alone, like odors, tastes, colors, etc. No, for as qualities these latter fall under the category of quality in Aristotle's scheme. Again, the so-called common sensibles are also in the category of quality. But the intellect is certainly not confined to apprehending only qualities, but rather is capable of apprehending anything and everything in whatever category it may be—substances, quantities, relations, times, places, actions, passions, etc., as well as qualities. Indeed, Aristotle speaks of the intellect as "the place of forms," [7] precisely in the sense that it is receptive of any and all forms in whatever category.

Under such circumstances, therefore, the intellect could not possibly be restricted to what can be received through a bodily organ like the eye or the ear or the nose or what not, these organs being receptive only of such qualities as can be materially received in that organ, like colors in the eye, or sounds against the eardrum, or flavors on the tongue. Instead, the intellect, insofar as it is receptive of forms, is not limited to what it receives through any organ, but rather is completely open to any and all forms. And as open or receptive to all forms indiscriminately, it would seem that the intellect itself must be bare of all forms, even characterless, so as to be thoroughly transparent or purely receptive. Were it to have any determinate forms or features in its own right, its reception of forms would then be as if through a sort of distorting medium. So it is that Aristotle understands his own characterization of the intellect as the place of forms, as meaning that the intellect as such is but a potentiality for any and all forms, in the sense that there is no form whose imprint the intellect cannot receive, at the same time receiving it, as we have said, but immaterially and intentionally.

Moreover, given that forms are in such wise received into the intellect, then there will be no problem at all as to how such forms can be, simply *qua* forms, one and the same with the forms of things that thereby come to be known. For be it a tree, a toad, a color, a spatial relation, a moment of time, or an action such as swimming or flying, the forms of such things as such—the what-it-is-to-be a toad, or the what-it-is-to-be a relation such as "north of," or what not—will be in no wise different as forms, whether they be received in the intellect, or whether they be in the things or entities in the world of which they are the forms. And so it is that that second main requisite of cognition is met in the case of intellectual knowledge, no less than in sensory cognition: the actual form in the intellect or in the sensory faculty is formally identical with the actual form as it is in things in the world.

One thing, however, is still lacking in this account, particularly of intellectual cognition. For even supposing that we have made provision for both of the requisite features of cognition—that the forms must be received in the knower and that such forms in the knower must be the same as those very forms as they exist in things—it still remains for us to provide some sort of causal account of the actual processes of coming to know. In the case of intellectual cognition, this comes down to explaining how it is that the forms of things come to be received in the intellect: what, in fact, is the agent of such a change from the intellect's being merely capable of receiving a given form immaterially or intentionally, and its actually receiving it? Now the case of sensory cognition scarcely offers any comparable problem. For it is the sensory quality itself, which, in being transmitted to the organ, serves as the agent that activates the sensory faculty or power. To put it rather crudely, it is no less than the red color itself that is conveyed to the eye that is the agent that activates the faculty of sight and causes it to receive this same form, but without the matter.

But with intellectual cognition, it can no longer be the case that it is the very form that is received that is itself the agent or efficient cause of the reception. For one thing, as we have already remarked, intellectual cognition is not dependent upon a form's actually being present in the sense organ. Consequently, whereas I cannot possibly see a patch of red color unless it is actually there before my eyes, I can perfectly well think of red or have a notion or concept of red without any red object present at all. Of course, it is true, as we all know on a common-sense basis, that in addition to actual sense presentations there are also such things as memory images, and even images that we conjure up ourselves. Thus I can perfectly well remember the red of the sky as it was in the evening day before yesterday; or I can simply imagine a red sky at evening. Such images are obviously not dependent upon any sense qualities actually being present to our sense organs at the time we call up or entertain such images in our mind's eye. In fact, it is for this very reason that in Aristotle's psychology he distinguishes explicitly between the so-called external senses on the one hand and what he calls the fantasy or the imagination on the other.

Still, even though such images as are the products of our imaginations are not dependent upon the actual presence of sense qualities in our sense organs, all such images differ from ideas and concepts, which are proper to intellectual cognition, in that the former are always particular, while the latter are universal. That is to say, any image that I may have of red is always of a particular shade of red, of a more or less determinate size and shape, etc. In contrast, my concept of red involves no more than the form of redness itself, abstracted from any and all particular objects that might happen to be red, or from any particular shade of red, or from any shape of size, that a given shade of red might happen to have, etc.—in other words, just redness itself.

Accordingly, the question as to the agent of intellectual cognition reduces for Aristotle to the question as to who or what it is that serves first to abstract such forms from their concrete association with other forms in the images that are presented to us both in sensation and in imagination, and then to impress them upon a recipient or potential intellect. In other words, it is from images and only from images that our intellectual cognition must arise, the reason being that there is no other way in which human knowers can ever come into cognitive contact with the forms of things, save through the senses and through the images that are constructed out of such original sense contents. At the same time, whereas in images forms are presented to us as particular—that is, as associated and fused with countless other forms in concrete particular images—in concepts the forms have been abstracted and separated out, and so are presented to us as no longer particular but as universal.

To explain how such universal ideas or concepts arise in the mind, Aristotle simply postulates a so-called agent intellect, as over against what we have already described as being the potential or receptive intellect. Nor does Aristotle say much about the actual agency of this agent intellect,[8] other than to suggest that it functions as a sort of light, playing upon the confused images of things and making possible the discrimination and the separating out of the pure forms from the images in which they are presented, all mixed up and confounded. Once abstracted and distinguished, the pure forms are then impressed upon the potential intellect by the active or agent intellect.

What, Then, of the Nature of Man
and of the Human Soul?

In the somewhat involved and tortuous sections preceding, it may indeed have struck many a reader that we have tended rather to lose sight of what was originally an indispensable part and parcel of the project of this chapter as a whole. What is the nature of things animate and of things human? Aristotle's answer to both parts of this question, we said, was obtained through his notion of the soul. For living things are none other than substances possessed of souls or psyches; and a human being, in turn, is only a substance with a distinctive kind of soul, namely, an intellectual or rational soul. To say that a substance has a rational soul is to say that it is informed by a substantial form which is at once the formal, final, and efficient cause of what are the characteristic human functions and activities—not only functions like nutrition, growth, and reproduction, which men share with plants, as well as the functions of sensation and locomotion, which they share with animals; but also those functions which are distinctive of and peculiar to men, rational knowledge and cognition.

Unfortunately, in the account which we have given of the human soul and of its cognitive functions, one might wonder if we may not have gone back upon, or perhaps even betrayed, that initial and basic account which we represented Aristotle as having given of the soul in general. For the soul in Aristotle's eyes was not to be regarded as a substance in its own right, or as a kind of motor attached to the body, but rather as a mere form of the body, and more specifically as a form in virtue of which the body is the particular kind of body that it is, and so able to perform the characteristic functions that are appropriate to it. In other words, the soul would seem to be no more than what a certain kind of body is, its essence, in effect, or its determinate nature. Surely, though, the human soul, involving as it does both an agent intellect, as well as an intellect that is receptive of forms, would seem to be rather more than merely the substantial form or determinate nature of a certain kind of living body. If anything, it sounds as if it would almost have to be a substance in its own right and one that was capable both of acting and being acted upon.

It's true, as we have already seen, that Aristotle so conceives of his substantial forms as to vest them each with its own proper agency or efficacy. Thus fire, as a light body, tends, simply in virtue of its substantial form, toward the periphery of the universe. Likewise, it is the substantial form or nature of a plant that causes it to grow and develop, and not any external force acting upon the plant from the outside. Nevertheless, in the latter case, insofar as the soul is thus active and efficient, what it acts upon is the matter or body of the plant, so as to effect changes in it—in its matter—thereby causing it to grow and develop.

Contrast, with all of this the sort of thing that Aristotle considers to take place in the case of intellectual cognition: it is not the material body which is acted upon by the agent intellect, so as to change it (the body) from being only a potential knower to being an actual knower; rather it is the passive or potential intellect that comes to be acted upon; and, far from being either an organ or part of the body, Aristotle insists—for very good reasons but still in a way that would seem hardly reconcilable with what he says about the relation of soul and body in general—that the potential intellect is not material at all, but purely immaterial. Would this not, then, seem to suggest that the human rational soul, so far from being a mere form of the body—or more generally a mere substantial form that cannot exist apart from the matter which it informs or determines—is, instead, an immaterial substance in its own right, which, however much it may be attached to or connected with a human material body, is nevertheless independent of it? In any case, such is the conclusion which Aristotle himself draws in a most cryptic and highly enigmatic passage in Book III, chapter 5 of the *De Anima*;

> When mind [or intellect or reason] is set free from its present conditions it appears as just what it is and nothing more; this alone is immortal and eternal (we do not, however, remember its former activity because, while mind in this sense is impassible, mind as passive is destructible), and without it nothing thinks.[9]

Such, indeed, is a translation of Aristotle's very words. But what may they be taken really to mean? Well, we certainly don't propose to allow ourselves to be trapped in the thickets of interpretation to which this baffling passage has given rise. Suffice it only to say that while one can perhaps appreciate the considerations, especially with respect to the phenomenon of human knowledge, that ultimately led Aristotle to this somewhat guarded and perhaps even reluctant acknowledgement of the immortality of the human soul, it is nevertheless not easy to see how the notion of an immortal soul is readily reconcilable with his general account of souls as mere substantial forms. Thus in his physics, for example, Aristotle believes that water is capable of being changed into air, and air into water. Further, since these for him are among the four elements, any change from the one into the other must be a substantial change; the matter which at one time is determined by the form of air is but prime matter, which subsequently comes to take on the form of water. In other words, it is a case of a purely material potentiality being now determinate in one way and now in another. Clearly, though, neither Aristotle nor anyone else would ever say that any such mere determination of a thing to be of this sort rather than that could survive the destruction and dissolution of the thing that had been thus rendered determinate in that particular way. Yet at the beginning of his treatise on the soul Aristotle insists that the soul is to be thought of as only the sort of thing that is related to the body simply as form (that is, a substantial form) to matter. Can he, then, be consistent when he goes on to suggest, toward the end of the same treatise on the soul, that the human rational soul, or at least that part of it which is the agent intellect, can exist without matter and so lay claim to a kind of immortality?

Chapter IV

Varieties of Human Achievement:
Ethics, Politics, Poetics, and the Arts

What if Aristotle were confronted with the Psalmist's question, "What is man that thou art mindful of him?" Surely, he would answer characteristically, saying that man is a rational animal. At once, many would probably think such an answer to be so hackneyed, not to say overly simple, as to be almost a nonanswer. Even if Aristotle were to elaborate upon his simple answer, one would still not be likely to hear a word about brain cells, or amino acids, or the double helix, or anything of the sort. Nor would this be only because a fourth century Greek would not have heard of such things, but because, even if Aristotle were to hear of them and were also to appreciate their relevance and importance to the question of what is man, he would nevertheless insist that in any attempt to understand man, or human life and human existence, one must take particular precaution against losing sight of the main highway for all of the innumerable side roads that contemporary biologists and biochemists are constantly directing our attention to. Thus whatever may be the chemical or anatomical or neurological features of the human body, what Aristotle would want to insist upon is that it is the soul or form or psyche that informs and animates all of these and orders them according to their distinctively human functions in a human being. Moreover, the distinctive character that the human soul or human substantial form gives to the life of the human body lies precisely in the fact that such a being turns out to be a corporeal being that is no less capable of knowledge and understanding.

Nor, surely, is this so far out of line with our ordinary, everyday approach to our fellow human beings, or with our common-sense presuppositions in dealing with them and thinking about them. Even when we sometimes accuse people, and perhaps even ourselves, of shamefully treating human beings as no better than dogs, or maybe even as no better than stocks and stones and senseless things, we still recognize that these are figures of speech, and that in fact no person in his senses is going to mistake a man for a dog, much less for a stone or mere senseless thing. In short, men are rational animals. That's the sum and substance of it, nor is there any getting around it, or away from it, or even beyond it.

Still, our concern to understand human life and human existence, to say nothing of our fellow human beings both individually and collectively, is a concern that is scarcely satisfied by any mere knowledge that man is a rational animal, or a being who can think and know and understand. Rather, what we want to get at is some understanding of how a being of such a nature may be expected to act and behave, what he will do, and how he will live. Indeed, we have already seen how in the *Physics* Aristotle's pervasive concern was with the changes of things, and more specifically with the characteristic patterns of change and modes of development of different kinds of things.

What pattern of development or type of activity, then, may we associate with the kind of being that is not just an animal, but a rational animal? Thus while it is entirely proper that we should occupy ourselves with the most elaborate and varied researches into the changes that go on in the human embryo as it develops, or with the intricate processes of human growth and maturation, to say nothing of the complicated functioning of the human body once it has developed—what is requisite to its health, how to deal with the problems of disease, of aging, of death, etc.—still, there is a sense in which these chemical, biological, and physiological investigations do not acquaint us directly and immediately with men's lives and actions as distinctively human. In other words, what is distinctive about the behavior and conduct of a human being is that it is the behavior of an animal that is capable of either a genuine or a presumed knowledge of what he is about, and that is disposed to act on such knowledge, be it presumed or genuine.

How, then, are we to understand the behavior and conduct of such human beings, or of beings and substances of this rational kind? Ought we not to consider first of all, as a sort of norm or standard, what a truly intelligent behavior on the part of a human being necessarily involves? After all, would not such a procedure be like the practice that Aristotle generally follows in attempting to understand the development and behavior of animate or living things generally, and of any and all things in the natural world as a whole? It is only in the light of a standard of what might be called the perfect functioning or full flowering of a plant or an animal that we can determine in the case of an individual tree, say, or of a dog, or of a rosebush, or whatever, that it is diseased, or stunted in its growth, or somehow not functioning properly. Indeed, an understanding of things and of the way they are can be gained only through understanding their causes; and, as we have already seen, the soul or substantial form of a living being serves as the final cause, no less than as the efficient and formal cause, of the changes and developments that go on in substances of this kind.

The Final Cause of
Human Existence: Complications
in Understanding Its Import

What, specifically, is the final cause of human life and of human action, or, put a little differently, what is that standard of human life and existence by which the conduct and behavior of men may be judged to measure up or to fall short, and in what ways and to what degrees? No sooner is this question posed in this particular way than immediately two rather curious difficulties or complications seem to arise.

For one thing, many if not most contemporary philosophers, and nearly all contemporary intellectuals, would be simply appalled by the question. For surely, they would say, no enlightened man or woman of the twentieth century could possibly subscribe to the view that norms or standards of excellence—in this case of human excellence—actually exist in nature. It takes only the most cursory acquaintance with modern anthropology and sociology and psychology to realize that standards of excellence in regard to human beings are as various as the culture or the society or the community or even the individual who sets up such standards. Besides, is not everyone aware that values are not to be confounded with, or even approximated to, facts at all; and that, merely as a matter of logic, value judgments are never to be confused with factual judgments? Thus a knowledge of the facts of nature, however exhaustive, would not in the least indicate whether what is or is not the case either is or is not what ought to be the case. Moreover, to evaluate something by calling it good or bad, or right or wrong, is not at all the same as to describe a thing by calling it red or green, or fast or slow, or round or square, or whatever. Instead, judgments of the latter sort are quite properly classifiable as factual judgments or judgments of fact, whereas evaluative judgments, far from being judgments of anything that is true in fact, are rather judgments that merely reflect our various human reactions to or our feelings about what is actually the case. For all of these reasons, therefore, it is not merely incredible, it is even straightout illogical, that anyone should suppose there to be an actual final cause of human nature which could and does serve as a natural or factually grounded standard by which your conduct and mine, as well as the other man's, may all be adjudged.

Before we turn to a consideration of how Aristotle might undertake to respond to such objections to his notion of a real final cause of human conduct and development, we must first take brief note of a second complication that is closely connected with this first one. And this is that even if Aristotle should be able to establish that there is a proper *telos* or final cause of human behavior, then immediately upon establishing such a thing, the very character of his whole enquiry will take on an altogether different cast. If we were to use Aristotle's own terms, the enquiry would cease to be one of *physics* and would become one of *ethics* (and possibly of *politics* as well). Why this shift, though, and just what does it mean?

Be it remembered that for Aristotle physics embraces any enquiry into the nature of things—that is to say, into the natures of the various kinds of substances in the natural world, as well as into the various kinds of changes that are proper to these substances and are determined by their respective natures. Accordingly, any physical enquiry must take cognizance of the relevant final causes of natural substances, through which the characteristic changes and developments of these different substances may be understood. Not only that, but when such a physical enquiry concerns itself specifically with human beings, as one kind of natural substance among others, then, as we have already seen, such an investigation must fix upon the characteristic *telos* or end or goal of human life and human existence.

No sooner is such a final cause or standard of perfection of human life brought into focus than the whole character of the enquiry seems immediately altered. For one thing, when as physicists we concern ourselves with the *telos* of human development, it is hardly the same as when, again as physicists in Aristotle's sense, we concern ourselves, say, with the *telos* of a particular kind of plant or animal, or even with the *telos* of light bodies, say, as contrasted to that of heavy bodies. When as physicists we determine what the good or final cause is of human life, we can scarcely abstract from the patent and pressing fact that we, the physicists, are ourselves human beings, and that therefore to determine what the goal or *telos* is of human life is to determine what our own goal or *telos* is as human beings.

For another thing, it is very different for a human being to determine what the goal or final cause is of his life as a human being, than it would be, say, for a fish or a pine tree—to invoke a condition contrary to fact—to determine what the final cause might be of their respective lives or existences. Knowing what their respective natural ends are would make no difference to the fish or to the pine tree, for their natural development and their attainment of their natural ends is not conditional upon their knowing what those ends are. Instead, if the conditions are right and there are no adverse circumstances, then any nonrational natural substance such as a fish or a pine tree will automatically grow and develop so as eventually to achieve its natural end or goal of perfection. In contrast, when it comes to human beings, they being rational beings, and their natural end or goal being that of living intelligently (that is, living in accordance with such knowledge and understanding as they are able to achieve), there is no way in which such rational natural substances could ever attain their goals as human beings, except as they come to know and recognize what those goals are and thus deliberately set out to attain them.

So it is that no sooner do we determine what the final cause is of our own human existence, than physics, in Aristotle's sense, will quite properly give place to ethics, ethics being simply enquiry directed toward finding the ways and means for us to attain our natural end—or, in other words, for us to attain the good life, or the full and perfect life for ourselves as men and human beings. Moreover, such a switch from physics to ethics must not be understood as betokening a switch from one domain of scientific or philosophical investigation to another, as if, say, from having occupied ourselves with chemistry, we were now to turn our attention to botany, or as if, to use a more Aristotelian example, we were to shift our attention from the domain of physics to that of mathematics or to that of metaphysics. For Aristotle the difference between physics and ethics is no mere difference in the subject matter of our knowledge; rather, it is a difference in the very character and mode of our knowledge of that subject matter. As Aristotle would put it, it is a difference between a knowledge that is strictly *theoretical* (in the sense of the Greek word, *theoria,* which signifies simply a viewing or a looking) and a knowledge that is *practical* or *productive* (in the sense of the Greek words *praxis* and *poesis,* which signify respectively a doing and a making).

Applying this distinction, ethics is said to be a practical, and not a merely theoretical knowledge, in that, far from being a knowledge of what is so or what is the case, it is a knowledge of how to do something—of how to act and behave in a truly human way, of how to live, in short. Or, somewhat analogously, one might contrast the sort of knowledge that is proper to a doctor or a physician, as over against the knowledge of a biologist or bio-chemist. In the latter cases, what is aimed at is in principle simply knowledge, and nothing but knowledge, or knowledge for its own sake. But with the practising physician, his knowledge is a knowledge that aims at doing something or effecting something: at restoring his patients to health or at preventing disease among them. In fact, in any number of places Aristotle suggests that, considered as practical knowledge, the end of ethics is not knowledge but action; nor is the study of ethics—or of any of the productive or "poetic" sciences either, for that matter—ever directed toward mere learning, but rather always toward learning how to do something.

For that matter, we may specify still further the practical character of ethical knowledge by noting that it is a knowledge that is associated with desire in a peculiar way. Granting for a moment that there is a natural goal or *telos* of human life, then it is precisely that toward which we are all oriented and which we all desire and aim at. Ethical knowledge, as Aristotle understands it, is precisely such a practical knowledge of—to put it crudely—how to get what we want; it is a knowledge of the ways and means whereby we may attain our natural end and what we naturally desire. In fact, Aristotle even comments that what affirmation and negation are in the sphere of the intellect and reason, so are pursuit and avoidance in the sphere of desire.[1] Since ethical knowledge is a practical knowledge of the courses of action that we should choose in order to attain our end, this means that to make such correct choices in the sphere of ethics, it is necessary both that our judgments be true and that our desires be the right desires. Aristotle then continues:

> For here we are speaking of practical thinking and of the attainment of truth in regard to action. In contrast, when it comes to theoretical [or speculative] thought, which is not concerned with action or production, for such thinking to be functioning well or ill means simply that it attains either the true or the false. Of course, the attainment of truth is the function of any and all thinking, but of practical thinking its function is the attaining of such truth as is in accordance with right desire.[2]

There is still another feature of the practical knowledge that is proper to ethics, as contrasted with such theoretical knowledge as is proper to other sciences. Expressed in a modern terminology, one might say that theoretical knowledge is such as to involve truths that are universal and necessary. Why? Aristotle's answer is that the theoretical knowledge in physics and mathematics and metaphysics is a knowledge of "those things whose principles simply cannot be otherwise." [3] For example, that the sum of the angles of a triangle is equal to two right angles, or that any change must necessarily be a change *of* something *from* something *to* something else, or that it is impossible for the same thing both to be and not be, etc.—such principles clearly express not merely the way things are or happen to be in fact, but how they must be and could not be otherwise. In contrast, in the practical knowledge that one has in ethics, or in the productive knowledge that goes with the various arts and skills, one is obviously dealing with a knowledge of things that can be otherwise, and for the very reason that a practical or a productive knowledge is precisely a knowledge of how to do something or to bring something about—that is, of how to make things otherwise.

Since both a practical knowledge of what is to be done in a given concrete situation, and a productive knowledge of how one is to go about effecting or providing something under varying circumstances and conditions, are in the very nature of the case a knowledge that bears on what is particular and concrete and contingent, it cannot possibly be a knowledge that is universal and necessary and certain. Hence Aristotle protests against demanding the same exactness and precision in matters of ethics to be expected, for example, in mathematics. In fact, one may only require such exactness in a given scientific discipline as is appropriate to the subject matter with which it deals. Clearly,

> matters of conduct and expediency have nothing fixed or invariable about them, any more than have matters of health. [Hence but little]

precision [is] possible in dealing with particular cases of conduct; for these come under no science or professional tradition, but the agents themselves have to consider what is suited to the circumstances on each occasion, just as is the case with the art of medicine or of navigation.[4]

What the Final Cause
or Telos of Human Life Is

The argument of the foregoing section was that if there be such a thing as a goal or final cause of human existence, then no sooner would we come by a knowledge of it than we should find ourselves implicated in a rather different sort of cognitive enterprise. Rather than theoretical knowledge, it would be the so-called practical knowledge of ethics and politics that we would be pursuing. And yet that such a practical knowledge as is proper to ethics or politics should even be possible depends upon a prior recognition of what the *telos* or final cause is of human life. But is there any such thing?

Aristotle had no doubt that there is. Nor would he be in the least put off by all of the countless modern arguments about the inescapable relativism of our moral or ethical judgments or about any so-called logic of moral discourse which supposedly would make it mandatory that all our moral or ethical judgments be construed as in principle nonfactual. Instead, Aristotle would doubtless begin his rejoinder by invoking that simple fact of human experience, one that many today would write off as being little more than an empty tautology—the fact that all men seek happiness. True, the conceptions which men have of happiness may well be as various as the men pursuing it, some supposing that happiness lies in sensual pleasure, others that it lies in wealth or power, others that it consists in fame or reputation. Yet however they may construe happiness, whatever they believe it to be, surely it is a fact that all men do pursue it. For happiness means no more than satisfaction of our desires; and it is little more than a truism that all our desiring, seeking, wanting, and striving, is aimed at satisfying or fulfilling those very wants, needs, or lacks from which our desires and wishes may be presumed to proceed. Accordingly, to say that all men seek happiness is to say that all men desire the satisfaction of their desires, and this does seem to be no more than a tautology.

Nor does Aristotle himself lag behind in acknowledging that when one says that happiness is that end or goal of human life which all men are agreed upon and therefore seek after, one really hasn't said very much. As he remarks: "To say, however, that the Supreme Good is happiness will probably appear a truism; we still require a more explicit account of what constitutes happiness." [5] What Aristotle is suggesting is that there must be a final cause of human existence toward which a man's entire natural development and progress are oriented, much as an acorn might be said to be oriented toward the attainment of its own perfection and fulfillment in the full grown tree. Moreover, as the acorn is ordered to its perfection as a full grown tree in the sense of a potentiality being ordered to its proper actuality, so also a maturing, developing human being is ordered to his own fulfillment as a fully developed human personality, again exactly as potentiality is to actuality.

At the same time, there is a difference in the two cases, that a human being, being a rational animal, is one who is consciously aware, often painfully aware, of his own lacks and needs—which is to say of his own unfulfilled potentialities. In consequence, a human being's life is not only shot through with desires, drives, and strivings of all kinds, but particularly of conscious desires; and one might even say that the life of a man resembles one long, sustained, conscious, deliberate, and yet multi-directed effort to fulfill his multifarious needs and potentialities. Hence if one may properly speak of a man's truly achieving what he aims at, in the sense of a fulfillment or completion or perfection of his life as a human being, then the attainment of such a thing will amount to the actualization of his potentialities, and as such will constitute what is indeed his true satisfaction and happiness. In trying to determine what it is that is man's natural end and perfection, Aristotle is really looking for what might be called an objective standard of human happiness, such that the failure and dissipation and wrong-headedness of so many men's lives may be recognized as being often due to their never having understood what their true happiness must consist in. It is quite possible even that many who think themselves happy, and who give every appearance of being altogether smug and self-satisfied in their own petty achievements, are really not happy at all. Such would be the consequence of there being an objective distinction between true happiness and only thinking or supposing oneself to be happy.

Still, is there any such objective standard of human happiness to be found? Or is there any such thing as a natural goal of human existence which properly represents the fulfillment of man's potentialities? Yes, Aristotle says, and the way to determine what it is is

by ascertaining what is man's function. For the goodness or efficiency of a flute-player or sculptor or craftsman of any sort, and in general of anybody who has some business or function to perform, is thought to reside in that function; and similarly, it may be held that the good of man resides in the function of man, if he has a function.

Are we then to suppose that, while the carpenter and the shoemaker have definite functions or businesses belonging to them, man as such has none, and is not designed by nature to fulfill any function? Must we not rather assume that, just as the eye, the hand, the foot and each of the various members of the body manifestly has a certain function of its own, so a human being also has a certain function over and above all the functions of his particular members? What then precisely can this function be? The mere act of living appears to be

shared even by plants, whereas we are looking for the function peculiar
to man; we must therefore set aside the vital activity of nutrition and
growth. Next in scale will come some form of sentient life; but this too
appears to be shared by horses, oxen, and animals generally. There
remains therefore what may be called the practical life of the rational
part of man.[6]

If this concluding and decisive phrase, "the practical life of the
rational part of man," does not come through too clearly, what
Aristotle means by it is nonetheless simple enough. He means
merely that man's proper function or activity is not simply one of
having intelligence in the sense of a certain I.Q., which one can
then show off upon occasion, but rather in the sense of actually
being intelligent in the living of one's life and of actually using
one's intelligence in making the day-to-day decisions of one's life.

Besides, does it not make sense, what Aristotle is here saying,
(1) that man's function, or man's perfection or full-development,
does indeed consist in no more and in no less than in his living in
the manner of someone with knowledge and understanding, and
(2) that it is just this end that all men do strive for and that is
consequently the source of their true happiness and satisfaction, if
only they would stop to consider as much? For as regards (1),
would we not all acknowledge that however healthy or fully
developed a human being might be in a narrowly physical or
biological sense, and however well he might be provided for in his
ordinary needs and desires, if in general he acted and behaved in a
way that was no better than a fool, we should hardly say that such a
person's existence was quite what we would consider to be a full or
proper existence for a human being. Similarly, as regards (2),
imagine yourself in a situation where you would be offered all of the
usual and perhaps unusual necessities and even goods of life—food,
clothing, housing, medical care, sex, and in general the so-called

creature comforts of every kind—but at the price of the loss of your awareness, would you settle for such an existence, and would you say that it would be your idea of true happiness and satisfaction? Or better still, suppose that you were offered all this, but not at the price of being totally unconscious, merely at the price of not having any genuine knowledge or understanding either of yourself or of the nature of things generally—that is to say, at the price of your not asking any questions, of your not raising any doubts, and so of your not really knowing the what or the why of anything. Would you settle for this? Presumably not.

But, then, is not Aristotle right in his insistence that the good or final cause of human life is precisely the intelligent life, and that the good of man, as well as man's true happiness, will consist simply in living wisely and intelligently, and with true understanding and discernment? Of course, to live intelligently is a somewhat different affair from carrying out intelligently various other of our characteristic human activities, such as, for example, building a house, trying a case, flying a plane, curing a patient, commanding an army, or what have you. For while these latter all require intelligence for their proper exercise, and are therefore activities which only intelligent beings can perform, being such as to require a certain skill or know-how, they nevertheless do involve rather less than what is involved in those day-to-day wise and intelligent choices that go to make up the life of a wise and intelligent man. For to live wisely means actually wanting to do so and choosing to do so, whereas in the case of ordinary skills and technical know-how, it is really no reflection upon a man's skill whether or not he chooses to exercise that skill, or enjoys exercising it.

With the skilled musician or the skilled accountant, for example, if he happens not to enjoy his work or even refuses to perform at all, he is no less a good musician or good card-player or good accountant for all of that. He still has the skill, whatever may be his likes or dislikes, his inclinations or disinclinations in the matter. Contrast the situation in regard to morals or ethics, where the question concerns someone's being a good man, as over against his being merely a good accountant, or good musician. Suppose that a man knows what the right course of action is in a given case—say, that of exercising his generosity, or being willing to face up to dangerous or unpleasant consequences, or being courteous and considerate to his fellow human beings, or being fair or honest in his dealings—and still, despite his knowledge of what he ought to do, either he doesn't do it, just because he doesn't want to; or he does it, but does it grudgingly or unwillingly, and perhaps merely out of fear of public disapproval or maybe out of no more than a hope of currying favor or getting ahead or out of other extraneous motives. Would we call such a man a good man, or, more specifically, a generous or courageous or courteous or just man? Surely not, for in moral matters, as contrasted to matters of art or know-how, a mere knowledge of what needs to be done or ought to be done is not enough; in addition, the person must actually do it, and do it from his own choice, and because he sincerely desires to do the right thing, or (more specifically) the generous thing, or courageous thing, or just thing, as the case may be.

So for Aristotle, the final cause of human existence, the achievement of the good life or the intelligent life, is not merely a matter of right knowledge or know-how—although it is at least that. But it is also a matter of right desire and of choosing the right, and choosing it for its own sake. Consequently, as Aristotle sees it, for a man to live intelligently is not merely an affair of what he calls in his technical language, "intellectual virtue"—the virtues of skill and know-how when it comes to determining what needs to be done or ought to be done. No less is it an affair of so-called "moral virtue"—such being the virtues of choice, through the acquisition and possession of which a man may come consistently to want and prefer just those courses of action which reason dictates as requisite and needing to be done.

Nor again does one need do more than appeal to common-sense considerations in confirmation of this view that intelligent behavior is entirely dependent on moral virtue. How many of us, how many times, have been in situations where we have realized perfectly well that what is called for is a generous expenditure on our part of time or money or effort in a particular social or community enterprise, but have held back for no other reason than that we were too lazy, or too taken up with less important things, or perhaps too loath to give any time or spend any money? Or who has not had the experience of giving way to anger or losing his temper, and so of doing what he otherwise knows to be exceedingly foolish or unwise things? Or is there anyone who at times may not have neglected to speak out when he ought to have spoken out, or who may have failed to stand up and be counted when he needed to, or who may even have betrayed a trust or a promise, simply because he was afraid—afraid of social pressures, or perhaps of loss of money, or maybe even of personal physical harm?

Now what all such examples point to is a simple fact of life, which is that our desires—and more generally our feelings, passions, emotions, impulses—are not always, and perhaps are only seldom, in line with our own better judgments as to what needs to be done or what it is incumbent upon us to do in particular concrete cases. Thus for this reason Aristotle stresses the absolute indispensability to the good life or the intelligent life of the cultivation and exercise of the so-called moral virtues. Nor, indeed, are these moral virtues anything but learned habits of choice, by which our actual choices will be made in accordance with such knowledge and understanding of the concrete situation as we may happen to have, instead of being deflected therefrom through fear or anger or greed or lust or envy or stinginess or pleasure or what not. In fact, Aristotle simply provides a classification of the moral virtues according to his classification of desires and passions. Doubtless today we might find ourselves disposed to classify such feelings and emotions rather differently from Aristotle. But whatever we may think of his over-all scheme of the virtues, his actual analysis and account of the way the various moral virtues operate has an inescapable plausibility about it.

Take a crude example, say that of a man's very common and natural love of wealth and possessions. As Aristotle sees it, there is nothing wrong with such a desire as such—or for that matter with any of our feelings or desires or emotions. Yet at the same time, we not infrequently judge such a love or desire, whether our own or the next man's, to be excessive, approximating perhaps to parsimony or even greed. On the other hand, there is the other extreme of not caring enough about our possessions or property or general means of sustenance, even to the point of being downright careless and prodigal in such matters. Accordingly, as Aristotle sees it, what we need to cultivate with respect to such natural inclinations as the desire for or love of wealth and possessions is the moral virtue of generosity, as a result of which we shall be disposed to choose what our better judgment prescribes to us as being in a mean between the excesses of illiberality on the one hand and of prodigality on the other.

Or again, take anger or fear. Surely, there is nothing wrong with either of these emotions as such. Yet it is something of which we are all painfully aware that through an excess either of fear or of anger or of both, we often do things which we may later seriously reproach ourselves for and recognize to have been both ill-judged and ill-timed. On the other hand, it is no less true, though perhaps less frequent, that men may manifest a deficiency in their anger or their indignation; and surely we have all known people who are rash and foolhardy. So once again, it is moral virtues of the type of courage and of, say, even-temper, that we need to cultivate, in the hope that rather than being given to excessive anger or ill-temper, or perhaps to excessive rashness, we can learn to be either angry or fearful, as the case may be, of the right things and at the right time and in the right amount. Such, then, is what it takes if as men we are to live wisely and intelligently, realizing that the perfection and function of human beings consists precisely in our bringing our rational knowledge and understanding to bear directly upon the course of our daily lives.

The Practical Business
of Living Intelligently

Already we have had occasion to note that Aristotle explicitly denies that ethics is an exact science, certainly not like mathematics, and not even like physics or metaphysics. Insofar as ethics is properly a science or knowledge at all—for it is indeed that, Aristotle would insist—it is a knowledge that bears on the particular concrete case, determining whether it is better that right here and now I should do this or that, or whether the wise course of action for me to follow would be along this line or that. Now obviously in concrete, particular matters like these, Aristotle would say it is impossible that my judgment as to what ought to be done should be either universal or necessary or certain.

Before we attempt to illustrate how such concrete practical judgments are able to be made in ethics and how they may legitimately lay claim to a kind of truth and knowledge all their own, even though it be not a universal truth or a certain knowledge, it might be well if we were first to guard against a possible misunderstanding. To say that ethics is an affair of practical knowledge, and that practical knowledge bears only upon instances that are particular and contingent, must still not be taken to mean that there are no universal principles in ethics. Quite the contrary. The very account in the preceding section of what man's natural end is, and of how the perfect functioning of man—and in this sense the very happiness and well-being of man—must consist in the exercise of both intellectual and moral virtues—all of this, Aristotle would say, is a knowledge that is at once universal and necessary. It is simply a knowledge of what man is in his very nature, and of what the final cause necessarily is of that distinctive sort of perfective or developmental change that pertains to human beings. In this sense, then, such a knowledge of man's true end, and of that which constitutes the good or perfection of human nature is no less universal and necessary as knowledge than would be, in Aristotle's eyes, a knowledge of the natures and natural ends of other things in nature—of plants, of animals, of the heavenly bodies, of the four elements, etc.

So it is that that practical knowledge which is characteristic of ethics, and which is a knowledge that bears on what is contingent and particular, is nonetheless a knowledge that rests upon principles that are by no means particular and contingent. But let us see if we cannot get a somewhat clearer idea of just how such practical knowledge can actually serve as a guide for us in the practical concerns of our lives. We can do no better than to introduce this topic by quoting a passage from Sartre. Sartre is directly concerned with denying that there is any such practical knowledge at all, or, for that matter, that there is any knowledge of any kind that is relevant to the rightness or wrongness of any of our choices or decisions in life.

> To give you an example . . . I shall cite the case of one of my students who came to see me under the following circumstances: his father was on bad terms with his mother, and, moreover, was inclined to be a collaborationist; his older brother had been killed in the German

offensive of 1940, and the young man, with somewhat immature but generous feelings, wanted to avenge him. His mother lived alone with him, very much upset by the half-treason of her husband and the death of her older son; the boy was her only consolation.

The boy was faced with the choice of leaving for England and joining the Free French forces—that is, leaving his mother behind—or remaining with his mother and helping her to carry on. He was fully aware that the woman lived only for him and that his going off—and perhaps his death—would plunge her into despair. He was also aware that every act he did for his mother's sake was a sure thing, in the sense that it was helping her to carry on, whereas every effort he made toward going off and fighting was an uncertain move which might run aground and prove completely useless; for example on his way to England he might, while passing through Spain, be detained indefinitely in a Spanish camp. He might reach England or Algiers and be stuck in an office at a desk job. As a result, he was faced with two very different kinds of action: one, concrete, immediate, but concerning only one individual; the other concerned an incomparably larger group, a national collectivity, but for that very reason was dubious, and might be interrupted en route. And at the same time, he was wavering between two kinds of ethics. On the one hand, an ethics of sympathy, of personal devotion; on the other, a broader ethics, but one whose efficacy was more dubious. He had to choose between the two.

Who could help him choose? Christian doctrine? No. Christian doctrine says "Be charitable, love your neighbor, take the more rugged path, etc. etc." But which is the more rugged path? Whom should he love as a brother? The fighting men or his mother? Which does the greater good, the vague act of fighting in a group, or the concrete one of helping a particular human being to go on living? Who can decide *a priori?* Nobody. . . .[7]

If values are vague, and if they are always too broad for the concrete and specific case that we are considering, the only thing left for us [might be just] to trust our instincts. That's what this young man tried to do; and when I saw him, he said, "In the end, feeling is what counts.

I ought to choose whichever pushes me in one direction. If I feel that I love my mother enough to sacrifice everything else for her—my desire for vengeance, for action, for adventure—then I'll stay with her. If, on the contrary, I feel that my love for my mother isn't enough, I'll leave."

But how is the value of a feeling determined? What gives his feeling for his mother value? Precisely the fact that he remained with her.[8]

. . . In other words, the feeling is formed by the acts one performs; so, I can not refer to it in order to act upon it. Which means that I can neither seek within myself the true condition which will impel me to act, nor apply to a system of ethics for concepts which will permit me to act. You will say, "At least, he did go to a teacher for advice." But if you seek advice from a priest, for example, you have chosen this priest; you already knew, more or less, just about what advice he was going to give you. In other words, choosing your adviser is involving yourself. The proof of this is that if you are a Christian, you will say, "Consult a priest." But some priests are collaborating, some are just marking time, some are resisting. Which to choose? If the young man chooses a priest who is resisting or collaborating, he has already decided on the kind of advice he is going to get. Therefore, in coming to see me he knew the answer I was going to give: "You're free, choose, that is, invent." No general ethics can show you what is to be done; there are no omens in the world. The Catholics will reply, "But there are." Granted—but, in any case, I myself choose the meaning they have.[9]

To this Sartrian position Aristotle would no doubt respond by agreeing with it—but only in part. He would certainly say that as regards most concrete moral questions, and certainly as regards this particular one, no one can ever decide them purely *a priori*. The complexities of the particular case are always such that to try to say in advance what should be done is almost certain to leave out at least some of the relevant features which one cannot possibly know about, save when one is confronted with the actual situation oneself and as it is right here and now. Even for someone else to tell you what you ought to do would be no less likely to involve overlooking at least some factors in the situation which only the agent himself could appreciate from his particular standpoint within the actual situation.

Be it noted, though, that this sort of tentativeness and uncertainty with respect to what ought to be done in the particular case is by no means peculiar to situations that call for moral decisions. Very much the same conditions often prevail in situations that do not call for any sort of moral decision at all, but only for a decision involving skill or technical know-how. Thus suppose, to take a rather trivial case, that a skilled game-fisherman finds himself in a situation of the following kind. He is alone in a small rowboat, using an ordinary rod and reel for tackle, and has just hooked a large northern pike about thirty feet away. The fish is fighting and lunging at a great rate, but at the same time the wind has caught the boat broadside and is rapidly blowing it directly into a large bed of lily pads. The fisherman is engaged with both hands on the rod and reel and cannot use the oars. He sees that if he does not land his fish quickly, both the fish and the line will soon become entangled in the pads and the fish will surely be lost. On the other hand, if he reels in too fast and does not play the fish with the utmost patience and caution, the fish is likely to break the line, and perhaps even the rod as well, and so get away. What is the fisherman to do?

Oddly enough, in this case, no less than in the case of Sartre's young man, there is no way of telling *a priori* what ought to be done. No fisherman friend on the shore, or possibly in another boat nearby, could possibly tell the first fisherman what to do. Supposing the first fisherman to be truly skilled in his art, he and he alone is in a position to judge the complexities of the actual situation; nor is anyone else in as favorable a position as he to make the necessary decisions and choices as to the best way to land the fish.

Let us push still a step further the analogy between the situation with which the fisherman is confronted and the situation with which Sartre's young man was confronted. Sartre wishes to make it clear that, objectively considered, there really is nothing in that situation, at least as it presents itself, that would enable the young man or anyone else in similar circumstances to determine with any degree of certainty which would be the better (the morally better) course for him to follow. But so likewise in the case of the fisherman, it could well be that there was nothing in the actual situation facing the fisherman that could have provided him with any decisively reliable clues for deciding which would be the better course (the technically better) to follow in attempting to land his fish. Indeed, one could even suppose that another equally skilled fisherman in an exactly similar situation might decide to follow just the opposite course from that opted for by the first fisherman; and yet both of them might be equally warranted in their decisions, as judged by the very highest standards of the fisherman's art.

Yet notice how this comparison of the practical moral problem facing Sartre's young man with the purely nonmoral technical problem facing the fisherman serves to bring out one curious and seemingly dubious feature of Sartre's analysis of the former. From the fact that one cannot resolve the young man's moral problem either *a priori* or from the outside, or that there would seem to be no objective considerations of any kind that would enable the young man to determine with any degree of certainty that the one course of action really was better than the other, Sartre concludes that there is no such thing as moral knowledge at all, or what Aristotle would call practical knowledge. Yet would it not be odd if with respect to the fisherman one were to conclude that because in the given case there might be no way of determining with any degree of reliability which would be the better way to land the fish, there was therefore no such thing as a fisherman's art and no skill in fishing at all, and that even the most skilled fisherman would need to be adjudged really not one whit better, when it comes to landing a fish, than is the mere tyro who has never even had a rod and reel in his hand before? But that is fantastic!

But so also would Sartre's argument seem to be fantastic, if from the fact that particular cases calling for moral decision frequently pose serious moral problems, and that sometimes it seems impossible to decide with any certainty which is the morally better course to follow, Sartre were to conclude, as he actually does conclude, that therefore there is no such thing as practical moral knowledge at all. Indeed, one wonders whether in his very exposition of the case of the young man Sartre may not in places have belied his own thesis to the effect that there are never objective considerations as to what is morally better or worse that might serve to guide our choices, but that always it is our own arbitrary choices that first of all invest our courses of action with their seeming qualities of being either better or worse. Notice how, in recounting the feelings of the young man that would appear to be impelling him in the direction of joining the Free French, Sartre mentions his desire "for vengeance, for action, for adventure," and Sartre even characterizes the first of these as being "somewhat immature." But in fact, from Aristotle's point of view, and accepting for a moment Aristotle's basic moral principle that the good life is simply the intelligent life, one could well ask whether to allow a mere love of adventure or a desire for vengeance or a hankering after excitement to determine one's decision in such a case would after all be the sort of thing that a truly wise or intelligent man would allow to happen under the circumstances. Would not certain moral virtues seem to be called for here which might serve to moderate such mere desires for vengeance or for adventure in such a way as to prevent them from militating against a truly rational and balanced decision? And does not Sartre seem to imply as much almost inadvertently when he acknowledges the young man's desire for vengeance to have been "somewhat immature?"

Or again, is it not at least conceivable that in his counter desire to stay at home and to comfort his mother, the young man may not have been so much motivated by considerations of love and sympathy and filial obligation as by some cowardly fear at the prospect of death and by a deep-seated reluctance to bestir himself or to surrender the familiar comforts and security of his surroundings for the unknown risks and dangers of the Resistance? To be sure, from Sartre's description one cannot infer that such feelings were operative in the young man. Yet surely it is conceivable that they might have been; and if they had been, would not Sartre have had to recognize that such feelings would have been, if not exactly immature, then at least relevant in enabling one to determine that any decision which the young man might have arrived at based on them would hardly have been the decision of a fully intelligent and virtuous man? In other words, such circumstances of the young man's choice and of his actions would indeed have been "omens in the world" of such an action's being scarcely that of a man of true practical wisdom and intelligence. Nor would these omens have had this meaning and significance as a result of anyone's choosing to bestow such a meaning upon them. No, in themselves they give clear indication of being the sort of action that does not proceed from the proper exercise of what Aristotle would call the intellectual and moral virtues.

From Ethics to Politics and Poetics

At this point someone might well ask whether we have completely lost sight of our own chapter heading, which called for a discussion of Aristotle's *Politics* and *Poetics*, no less than of his *Ethics?*

Perhaps, though, as regards politics the omission is not so serious. For one thing, Aristotle's *Politics* is not a radical departure from, or even a marked development over and above the *Ethics*. One might even say that it is more of the same, at least as considered as a progression along an already determined and indicated line. Taking over from the *Ethics* the notion of the good life, or of the full development of a human being considered in respect to his capacity for being human, Aristotle considers the starting point of the *Politics* to be simply a recognition of the fact that integral to the fullness or perfection of any individual human life is a life lived in society or a life of political association (that is, in a *polis*). "Man," he says in a celebrated passage, "is by nature a political animal." [10] And indeed should there be any being who could be said to be by nature simply a solitary, or ἄπολις as Aristotle calls him, he wouldn't be a human being at all, but either a beast or a god.[11]

At the same time, however much Aristotle may have wished to insist that a human being cannot be truly human save in a political association, he would seem equally concerned to guarantee to the citizen of the *polis* what we might today call the rights of the individual, if not over against the political community, then indeed within that community. Thus he decisively repudiates Plato's communism, in which both private property and the family would be eliminated. In Aristotle's conception of distributive justice, it is in no sense the principle of to-each-according-to-his-needs-and-from-each-according-to-his-abilities that is the operative one, but rather the principle of to-each-according-to-his-deserts. He conceives of the ideal state or political community as being one in which all of the citizens will be, if not equal, then certainly not too unequal in their wealth, their birth, or their capacity and virtue. Hence each and every citizen will have a share in political power, such that each will take his turn now in governing and now in being governed, and with the result that by this means the end or goal of the political community may best be achieved—which is the common good, as contrasted to the good of any one class or group of citizens.

Moreover, the theme which recurs again and again throughout the *Politics* is one that may indeed sound strange to modern ears. Most of us nowadays are inclined. to assume that the purpose and function of the state is to make available to us various so-called external goods, hopefully in ever increasing amounts, and so to provide us with an ever higher and higher standard of living. But not so Aristotle, for his constant message is that the aim of the state is not so much to provide men with goods as to make them good men. And by "good" Aristotle means "morally good," which, in turn, he immediately construes in the sense already determined in the *Ethics*, where the good life for man is held to consist simply in the exercise of the intellectual and moral virtues.

If, then, Aristotle's *Politics* may be interpreted as less a development than a further deployment of the principles laid down in the *Ethics*, what about the *Poetics*? Is it similarly a treatise that is, as it were, in fief to the *Ethics*? Surely the answer to this question must be "Yes," and yet it is not an answer that most interpreters of Aristotle's *Poetics* tend to stress—and that for a very good reason. The *Poetics* represents a variety of discipline and a type of knowledge that is in principle quite different from that of either ethics or politics. These last, as we have seen, involve what Aristotle would call a practical knowledge, by which he means a knowledge of how to live and how to conduct oneself in a fully and properly human way in all of one's daily affairs both public and private. In contrast, "poetics" signifies the kind of knowledge that Aristotle would characterize as being rather productive than practical. And indeed the word *poetics* in its root meaning must not be thought of as confined to what we now call *poetry* and such things as are cognate with it. Instead, "poetics" is derived from a Greek word meaning to make or to fashion, so that all of the countlessly varied human activities associated with the various skills and crafts—shoe-making, house-building, cabinet-making, the medical art, military tactics and strategy, etc., etc.—are activities that might be labelled *poetic* in this broad sense.

Moreover, the contrast between these poetic arts, or arts of making, with the practical arts of ethics and politics, consists, Aristotle suggests, simply in this: in the practical arts the end or purpose of what one is doing lies in the very doing or activity itself—namely, living well or conducting oneself wisely and intelligently; in contrast, in the productive arts the end does not lie simply in the productive activity itself, but rather in the finished product that results from the activity—in the house in the case of house-building, or in the finished shoe in the case of shoe-making, or in the health of the patient in the case of medicine, etc. Consequent upon this contrast is the further and still more significant contrast which we have already touched upon in an earlier section. In the productive arts the only thing that counts, so far as our judgment of the artist's skill is concerned, is how well he does the job; whereas in ethics and politics, it is not just how well he does the job, but also the kind of a person the doer of the job himself is. If the end of medicine be simply the production of health in the patient, then so far as that end is concerned, it makes no difference whether the doctor himself be a saint or a scoundrel; all that matters is whether he have the requisite skill or know-how. But when it comes to living well—which is to say, being a good man or a good citizen—then it is no longer beside the point what kind of a person the man is; on the contrary, that is exactly the point!

Narrowing the notion of poetics from the general notion of making, or fabricating, or manufacturing, or creating no matter what, to the specific notion of the *Poetics*, where the concern is the making of poems, and more specifically the making or authoring of plays, and still more specifically of tragedies, how is such a making or authoring or producing to be understood? Aristotle's answer is that in the making or producing of a play or drama—or, more specifically, a tragedy—the making will consist in what is called an imitating or a representing ($\mu\iota\mu\eta\sigma\iota\varsigma$). What is it that will thus be imitated or represented? Aristotle's answer is that it will be an imitating or a representing of an action, and particularly a human action. But of course human action for Aristotle betokens moral action or, perhaps better, action of moral or ethical import. In any case, the actions that are re-presented in tragedies must necessarily be actions seen against the entire background of happiness as the end of human life, and of living intelligently as the very function or proper activity of human beings considered as rational and political animals.

Seen against this moral or ethical background, an action that is imitated or represented or enacted in a tragedy, is such an action as misses the mark, that is to say, it is an action that goes wrong, with the result that instead of contributing to or furthering the agent's well-being or happiness it militates against it and makes it impossible. That is just the tragedy of it. Besides, it being an action of moral or ethical import that is being enacted, the failure and tragedy of the action is not the sort of thing that need evoke no more than a purely dispassionate, indifferent judgment to that effect on the part of those who witness it. After all, an ethical judgment that a certain action is wrong is a judgment of a very different character, Aristotle would insist, from any purely theoretical judgment such as, say, that a certain number is a prime number. As we have already had occasion to note, it is a striking feature of Aristotle's ethics that ethics is not an affair of merely performing actions of a certain prescribed character: a man who performs just acts is not necessarily a just man, unless he himself loves justice and passionately desires it for its own sake.

So it is that even in the context and setting of the theatre, Aristotle insists that any poet or playwright who undertakes to imitate or exhibit an action of moral import like a tragic action must do so in such a way that the imitated action will evoke the proper response on the part of the audience. The response that is appropriate to a tragic action, Aristotle says, is a response alike of pity and fear. Not that the poet or playwright himself need necessarily feel this way about the action he is seeking to depict. True, should the poet be so morally insensitive as not to have such a reaction, then we might hesitate to call him a good man. But for him to be a good poet as such, his being a good man is irrelevant; rather all that is requisite is that his product be good—in this case a successful imitation or reproduction of a human moral action so as to evoke a response of pity and fear on the part of the spectators.

And now for one final caution. Let it not be thought—and Aristotle is most careful to guard against this—that when the talk is of an imitation or a re-enactment or reproduction of human action appropriate to tragedy, all that is meant is a mere re-telling or re-producing of human deeds of the sort that is usually associated with history. No, it is rather, as Aristotle remarks, that poetry is more philosophical than history; and by this he means that in poetry it is the universal, rather than the factual details, that the poet seeks to show forth. Perhaps we might construe this as meaning that it is precisely those universal and abiding features of our perennial human situation that it is the primary concern of poetry to exhibit, as contrasted with history.

At the same time, one might question whether it might not be ethics, as Aristotle understood it, and perhaps psychology or anthropology as well, that are much more directly and properly concerned with disclosing that which is universal and essential in man, far more than poetry is ever concerned with doing. To this, of course, the Aristotelian answer is "Yes." And yet the way in which the universal or the essential in regard to man is presented in tragedy is very different from the way in which it is presented in either ethics or psychology. In the latter the universal is abstracted from the particular, whereas in the former it is exhibited or enacted directly in the particular—that is, in a setting of the manifold and ever changing details of everyday practical life. In fact, it is here that the difference lies between poetry and science, in their respective efforts to mediate our understanding and appreciation of man and of our human situation.

A Final Tension: the Claims of Contemplation as Over Against Those of a Life of Moral Action

Here we must, alas, bring ourselves up sharp with a possible final qualification and reservation with respect to what might be called Aristotle's entire moral or ethical program, and consider this as embracing his discussions of politics and poetics as well. It has been thought by many to be ironical, if not a simple inconsistency, that having set forth with such care and detail and in so many places what he takes to be the nature and requirements of the moral life and of human ethical existence, Aristotle then appears—or at least so it has seemed to many—to take it all back in the tenth and last book of his *Ethics*. For there he seems to be saying that the good life or the happy life for a human being must consist finally not in moral and political action at all, or in the exercise of virtues like courage, temperance, generosity, justice, magnanimity, *et al.*, but rather simply in a supreme and, so far as possible, wholly uninterrupted activity of theoretical knowledge and pure contemplation.

Now why would Aristotle say this sort of thing, particularly after his having expended untold effort not only in the *Ethics* but elsewhere in attempting to characterize the life of man as being one of moral and political action, and thus hardly one of contemplation at all? Yet, consider that in Aristotle's eyes—and the same would at least up to a point be no less true from the standpoint of common sense as well—the distinctive thing about a human being is that he is an intelligent being, or a being capable of rational knowledge and understanding. But what, after all, is the point of knowledge and understanding? It is true that many of us think that the only reason for knowledge is what it can do for us, as if the only justification for scientific knowledge, say, were to lie in its import for technology. Or if it be not technology and the control of nature that are the point and purpose of knowledge, then why not think of knowledge as being relevant for the control of ourselves? This last would seem to be just the sort of thing that Aristotle throughout almost the whole of the *Ethics* appears to consider to be the prime desired consequence of knowledge, so far as human beings are concerned: knowledge makes it possible for men not merely to have knowledge, but to act upon it; not merely to be intelligent, but to live intelligently.

Nevertheless, tucked away in a somewhat obscure part of the *Ethics* is a most interesting question that Aristotle himself raises. Why not say that the chief if not the sole end of human knowledge is simply the knowledge of man? To which Aristotle's rather laconic answer is that man being anything but the most important thing in the universe, man therefore ought certainly not to be considered the most important object of knowledge in the universe, even of human knowledge. And why is not Aristotle's general line of thought on this score an eminently plausible one? For as we all would admit that an action such as war can only be for the sake of peace, so more generally why should we not say that all of our striving and struggle ought to be thought of as being for the sake of something beyond that struggle? Why not say, for instance, that all of the business of research and investigation in science, far from being an end in itself, is rather a means to the final end of simply knowing the truth, and knowing it for its own sake? Again, why not say that all of our practical knowledge in ethics and politics which could be the means of our eventually coming to live intelligently and in the manner of wise and virtuous men—why not say that over and above and beyond such a life of virtuous action there lies the still more ultimate end of our simply being able to contemplate the truth in a knowledge of God, of man, and of the whole nature of things?

It should not be forgotten that when we discussed earlier Aristotle's account of things animate and be-souled, and particularly the human soul, we found that there seemed to be a certain tension in his presentation. Initially, and throughout most of his account, the soul was to be understood as no more than the form of the body in the sense of being simply the determinate nature of the body, and in virtue of which the body is simply the kind of body that it is, a living body. But then when he came to the human soul, and more particularly to intelligence in men, Aristotle threw out certain cryptic suggestions that the intellect might well be immortal and so capable of a life of its own, no longer as the mere form or whatness of the human body. Returning then again to the *Ethics* and to the life of contemplation that seems to be recommended in the concluding book, ought it not to be recognized that it is just such a life of contemplation that would befit man's rational soul, at least insofar as it is separable from the body and so capable of a life independent of and so higher than that of the body?

Listen to Aristotle's own words on the matter:

> . . . whereas the activity of the intellect is felt to excell in serious worth, consisting as it does in contemplation, and to aim at no end

beyond itself, and also to contain a pleasure peculiar to itself, and therefore augmenting its activity. . . .[12]

Such a life as this however will be higher than the human level: not in virtue of his humanity will a man achieve it, but in virtue of something within him that is divine; and by as much as this something is superior to the exercise of the other forms of virtue. If then the intellect is something divine in comparison with man, so is the life of the intellect divine in comparison with human life. Nor ought we to obey those who enjoin that a man should have man's thoughts and a mortal the thoughts of mortality, but we ought so far as possible to achieve immortality, and do all that man may to live in accordance with the highest thing in him; for though this be small in bulk, in power and value it far surpasses all the rest.[13]

These words of Aristotle are nothing if not eloquent. Yet has he perhaps over-reached himself and betrayed what one might well call the earthy, naturalistic, down-to-earth bias of his philosophy as a whole and of his ethics in particular? Or is it that he is exploiting various hidden potentialities of that philosophy which he himself glimpsed perhaps none too clearly, but which many of his commentators and interpreters have altogether failed to see? We leave the question open.

Chapter V

After the Physics, Metaphysics

After the *Physics* what need could there be for a metaphysics? Could it be that there is some loose or left-over subject matter that has escaped treatment in physics and that ought now to be taken up in a metaphysics? As one turns to a reading of Aristotle's *Metaphysics*, particularly today, it is not unlikely that one will have questions of this sort in mind. Somewhat analogously in the contemporary philosophical scene—although it is always dangerous to think of Aristotelian science on the analogy of modern science—one finds oneself inclined to raise similar questions about contemporary science and philosophy. What is the specific subject matter that philosophy may be thought to be equipped to take up and treat of that the sciences have not already exhausted, or at least have not inscribed in their long-range program as something to be exhausted eventually by them and through the application of their methods?

And so likewise with respect to Aristotle. In the program of his physics, as Aristotle conceives it, there is nothing whatever in the natural world that is not properly to be thought of as being subsumable under physics—biology, astronomy, embryology, psychology, meteorology, these are all in Aristotle's eyes proper subdivisions of what he would call physics.[1] Thus it is physics that is supposed to inform us of the nature of things, and of anything and everything within the *natura rerum*. Where, then, is there room or place for metaphysics, or what Aristotle himself was wont to call *first philosophy*?

Of course, there are disciplines in the Aristotelian scheme like ethics, politics, poetics, etc., which quite recognizably fall outside of the domain of physics. As we have already had occasion to note, these "sciences" do not fall outside of physics because they treat of things that are nonphysical—things that are not subject to change or motion—but rather because as sciences their aim or their method, as Aristotle would put it, is not so much theoretical as practical or productive; that is, their aim is not exclusively one of knowing, but rather one either of doing or of making. In contrast, the particular discipline which Aristotle calls *metaphysics* is quite unmistakably a theoretical science. But then again the question becomes pressing as to what it is that such a so-called theoretical science as metaphysics can treat of, as contradistinguished from physics.

What Are We to Understand by Metaphysics?

Perhaps a clue to the answer may be found in the very associations most of us are likely to have with the word *metaphysics*. Does not the usual connotation of *metaphysics* suggest a concern with such things as may lie beyond (or perhaps even above) the domain of physics? And surely, Aristotle himself is wont on various occasions to contrast with one another the three different sorts of theoretical science—physics, mathematics, and metaphysics.[2] Moreover, the key to this three-fold division of sciences—or, one is tempted to say, to these three different kinds of "knowledges" [3]—is to be found in the differences in their respective subject matters, or in the differing kinds of things or objects that they are respectively concerned with. Thus physics is to be thought of as being concerned with material things, provided, of course, one is careful to understand *matter* or *material things* in the way Aristotle does, as being that which is subject to change or motion, rather than in the way we are accustomed to today as being that which occupies space and has weight. In contrast, mathematics, as Aristotle understands it, is considered to have a subject matter that is somehow ambivalent between the material and the immaterial. Thus, on the one hand, it would seem obvious that the objects of mathematics—things like numbers or quantities, or squares, circles, ellipses, etc.—can indeed have no existence in the real world, except as the amounts or dimensions of material things or substances. On the other hand, Aristotle recognizes no less clearly that even though such mathematical entities or subjects can never exist apart from matter, they can perfectly well be considered and treated of by the mathematician independently of their material conditions. Thus the circle as it is considered by a geometer is not the same, and is not subject to the same material conditions, as the circle that is drawn in the sand or on the blackboard. The latter is subject to being erased or washed away by the tide; it is bound to be of some color or other, say white on a black background, or a darker depression against a lighter expanse of sand; it is sure to be in varying degrees either illuminated by the light or else shaded from it, etc. In contrast, as considered by the geometer, the circle is simply abstracted from and considered in complete independence of any and all such material conditions.

But does not this very contrast between physical objects and mathematical objects suggest the possibility of still a third class of objects—those that are completely and unrestrictedly immaterial? Thus physics is concerned with such things as can neither exist apart from matter nor be conceived apart from matter. These are material things proper. Mathematics occupies itself with objects which, although they can certainly be conceived and understood apart from matter and material conditions, are nevertheless incapable of being or existing apart from matter. That leaves such things as can both be conceived apart from matter, as well as exist apart from matter—properly and completely immaterial things—as the fit objects or subjects of a discipline which, in contrast to physics, might be called a *metaphysics*?

Certainly, it is pretty much in this way that the term *metaphysics* tends to be understood by contemporary philosophers and writers who continue to use it. And oftentimes, since many of these same philosophers and writers are eminently secure in their convictions that there aren't any so-called immaterial things or objects at all, they are able immediately and confidently to conclude that there is no genuine science of metaphysics, or that it is at best only a pseudo-science. To be sure, it is another, albeit a next natural, question whether these same contemporary thinkers and writers may be inclined to push still further on and say that as metaphysics can no longer claim to be a legitimate discipline, simply because there are no nonphysical or immaterial objects lying beyond the domain of physics, so also philosophy itself can no longer claim to be a legitimate discipline. Since the entire domain of what Aristotle called physics, formerly the preserve of philosophers,[4] has gradually been taken over and now stands completely preempted by the various modern sciences, this last is, indeed, another question.

As to the question before us, concerning whether Aristotle felt that there was a legitimate science of metaphysics, and whether this science did concern itself with things immaterial, the answer must doubtless be a "Yes"; and yet it must also be a decidedly qualified "Yes." For one thing, the term *metaphysics* was never used by Aristotle himself, despite the fact that it is by the title of *The Metaphysics* (Τα μετα τα Φυσικα) that Aristotle's great work has come to be known; and despite the fact, too, that, in consequence of the tremendous influence which that work has had in the history of Western philosophy, Aristotle has himself come to be thought of in the minds of many as being the metaphysician par excellence. No, the curious historical fact—at least according to a long-standing scholarly tradition—is that the title, *The Metaphysics*, was a title given by a first century editor of Aristotle to those treatises in the Aristotelian corpus which came "after the physics" (a literal translation of μετὰ τὰ φυσικά). Moreover, it was long fashionable for scholars to think that this editor did not in any way intend by such a title to designate things which come after the study of physics in the sense of being somehow higher or nobler than mere physical things, much as the immaterial might be thought to be higher or nobler than the physical, or the supernatural than the natural: all that was meant was a mere label or designation for those of Aristotle's treatises that were ranged, as it were, on the shelf following the physical treatises.[5] Yet for all of that, the later connotations that have come to accrue to the expression "Aristotle's Metaphysics" are perhaps not an unreliable guide to the content of that work, however much they may have outrun the original intent and purpose of the literal designations of "after the physics."

There is another reason why it is only with a certain reserve that one ought to say that for Aristotle the term *metaphysics* signifies that science or investigation that concerns itself with the immaterial rather than the material. Quite apart from the fact that Aristotle himself never used the term *metaphysics* in this sense, it is also and on other grounds misleading to say that in metaphysics, or "first philosophy," Aristotle concerned himself exclusively with such things and entities as transcend the physical or lie beyond the domain of the physical. While it is true that in Book E of *The Metaphysics* Aristotle does say that the proper subject matter of this science must be no less than god himself or the gods, these being entities that exist apart from matter and are therefore eternal and immobile and imperishable (in short, the subject matter of metaphysics is here explicitly equated with that of theology), it is no less true that earlier on in Book Γ of the *Metaphysics* Aristotle apparently chooses to characterize the subject matter of metaphysics quite differently. This time it isn't a particular kind of being—god or the gods—that metaphysics investigates, but rather being as such, or being in general.

What, though, could this latter mean? Actually, despite the awkwardness and seeming artificiality and perhaps even emptiness of terms like *being as such* or *being*-qua-*being* or *being in general*, it is by no means difficult to get, shall we say, a kind of feel for the sort of thing that Aristotle is here about. It is the same sort of enterprise that any number of recent philosophers, as different from one another as Russell and Sartre, or as Bergmann and Sellars, have recognized to be more or less their common enterprise—an enterprise which, however much they might be reluctant to admit it, they also have in common with Aristotle. To characterize this enterprise in a somewhat rough and ready way, we might say that it is one that concerns itself with trying to determine what it takes for things to be or to be real; that is to say, what is it that is required in order that a thing may lay claim to being or to being something that really is or exists? Nor must this question be thought of as applicable to some one particular kind of being to the exclusion of all others. Rather with respect to anything and everything, we may properly ask what we may be supposed to mean when we say that that thing is or that it exists or is real: in virtue of what do we say that it is a being; what is it that constitutes it a being, or what is it that is requisite in order that the particular thing under consideration, or anything else for that matter, should be?

To take a rather crude example first, it is not uncommon to speak of someone as being a materialist in philosophy. A materialist is simply one who maintains that for anything to be or to exist it must be material. And being material might be further specified as being that which occupies space and has weight. Among those materialists who are at the same time atomists, it is further maintained that such matter exists, as it were, atomized—in ultimate, indivisible, and indestructible particles out of which anything and everything in the real world, be it fish or flesh or good red herring—is in the final analysis made up or composed, and into which it can ultimately be broken down or resolved. In other words, for an atomistic materialist what is requisite for anything to be or to exist is that it should be either a material atom itself or else compounded out of such atoms.

A different example might be taken from Plato, or at least from that somewhat over-simplified version of Plato's metaphysics that has frequently been associated with such middle-period dialogues as the *Phaedo* and the *Republic.* It is certainly not incorrect to say that Plato was profoundly impressed by the contrast between ordinary everyday objects and what might be called their natures, characters, attributes, or, as Plato would put it, the forms or "ideas" of those objects. Thus, a triangle drawn in the sand, say, is no doubt a triangle in some manner or other; and yet at the same time the actual triangle as it is drawn there in the sand is hardly to be confused with the very character of triangularity which that same actual triangle is recognized as having. Or put a little differently, the actual triangle is hardly the same as its own very nature of being a triangle, or as what it is to be a triangle. For while the triangle in the sand can be rubbed out or washed away, such destruction in no way affects or alters the character of being a triangle, or what it is to be a triangle. Indeed, triangularity or what-it-is-to-be a triangle are just the same, whether or not this, that, or the other triangle exists. And being thus always and ever the same, and never coming into being or passing away, it would seem that, whatever may be true of individual triangles, that sort of thing that we call *triangularity,* or the very nature or essence of being a triangle—this latter must surely be acknowledged to be immutable, imperishable, the same in all different triangles, and even the very norm or standard of perfection to which particular individual triangles can only approximate.

So impressed was Plato by such immutability and timelessness and perfection as attach to the natures or characters of things that, were he to have been confronted with the question of what does it take for a thing to be, or what is requisite to its very being, Plato would doubtless have unhesitatingly responded: for anything truly to be, it must be a Form or Idea—an eternal or immutable nature or essence or character. And suppose one were to cavil somewhat at this Platonic answer and to interject, "But surely, the many particular triangles that there are or have been or will be, and likewise the countless individual human beings, living or dead, to say nothing of all the other individual things past, present, or future, be they tables or chairs or stars or blades of grass or colors of the rainbow or what—surely all of these things cannot be denied being, but rather must be said to be or exist in their own fashion, no less than do the immutable Forms and Ideas." To this Plato would of course agree; yet he would hasten to add that if one were to ask what it takes for such things to be or what is requisite for their being, the answer would have to be: "They are able to be or to exist only in so far as they participate in or partake of the being of the Forms. For the being of the Forms is a being that is perfect and immutable, whereas the being of other things is only imperfect and partial and even borrowed or participatory, inasmuch as nothing whatever, be it triangles or men or dogs or relationships or what not, can possibly be or be what they are, save in so far as they participate in the true Form or nature of triangle, or of dog, or of man, or of relatedness, or what not."

So it appears that the basic answer that Plato would be inclined to give to a question such as "What does it mean for something to be?" or "What does it take for a thing to be?" would presumably be to the effect: "To be is either to be a Form, or at least to partake of some Form or Forms. The Forms, therefore, or the Ideas are the prime requisites for things to be or to exist."

Aristotle's Ontology as Distinguished from His Metaphysics

So much, then, by way of examples of how different thinkers have sought to answer the question of what being is, or what it takes for a thing to be. As we have already intimated, present-day thinkers tend to shy away from anything like "metaphysics," which is generally interpreted to signify a concern with that which lies beyond the physical; it therefore tends immediately to lose caste in the eyes of contemporaries on the ground that it is a discipline that must presumably outrun experience and must thus attempt to lay claim to a knowledge of that which is "trans-empirical" [6] and transcendent. On the other hand, when it comes to questions of what the being of things in the empirical world is, or what it is in respect to the real things of the world that makes them to be, or is the source or principle of their very being or reality, such questions are of deep concern to any number of contemporary philosophers. Yet rather than call such a discipline *metaphysics*, contemporary thinkers often prefer the word *ontology*, which means literally the science or study of being, and which as such is thought to be free of all associations with the transcendent and the trans-empirical. So far as Aristotle is concerned, it is rather curious that although the major part of his *Metaphysics* is taken up with what we today might prefer to call ontological investigations, he seems to feel no particular need to try to distinguish these sharply from his investigations concerned with entities that he takes to be wholly immaterial and nonphysical, and that therefore fall properly under his own label of being theological.

Be this as it may, let us now look to Aristotle's own ontology. Having got something of a feel for what are nowadays likely to be called ontological questions, let's see how Aristotle undertakes to answer his own questions as to what being is, or what it takes for something to be. At once Aristotle's answer comes through clearly and unequivocally: "And indeed the question which was raised of old and is raised now and always, and is always the subject of doubt, namely, what being is, is just the question, what is substance?" [7] If we may be permitted a hasty paraphrase, what Aristotle means is simply: "To be is to be a substance, or at least to be somehow associated with or dependent upon a substance."

Nor is it surprising that this should be Aristotle's answer. We have already had occasion not just to note but to stress the importance which Aristotle attaches to that elementary common-sense consideration that in our everyday world the manifold features, actions, characteristics, sizes, places, relations, etc. of things are just that: they are in or of things. In other words, there is no quantity but what it must be the quantity of something, no quality but what it is the quality of something, nothing is done but what there must be something that does it, no relations without things related. And what are these things that are thus quantified, thus qualified, thus related; moved from place to place; now active, now passive; now in this state or condition, now in that—what are these things? They are what Aristotle calls *substances*.

To be sure, in other and earlier contexts of his philosophy than that of the *Metaphysics*, Aristotle was interested in substance perhaps not so much for its prime ontological role as for certain other roles that it plays. Thus in the *Physics* Aristotle's concern was not with being *qua* being as in the *Metaphysics*, but rather with motion and change. Requisite, though, to any and all change, Aristotle insists, there must be something that changes; and that something in the case of quantitative and qualitative changes, as well as in that of locomotion, is always and necessarily a material substance. So also in the *Categories*, where Aristotle is concerned with logical questions, he notes that what he calls *primary substance* plays the distinctive role of that which can be neither predicable of nor present in a subject; that is to say, it is simply a fact of logic that individual substances—for example, John Jones or Socrates or you or I—are not and cannot be descriptive of anything else. Socrates, for example, is not anything with which you describe anything else. You can't say that the pen in my hand, or the dog down in the street, or this piece of paper, or anything else is Socrates. On the other hand, as Socrates cannot be used to describe anything, there are countless things that can be used to describe Socrates or can be predicated of him—that he was snub-nosed, that he lived in Athens, that he was the teacher of Plato, etc.

In other words, in logic substance plays the role of that which is always subject and never predicate, as in physics it plays the role of that which must necessarily underlie change or which undergoes or is subject to change. But now in the *Metaphysics* the concern is with ontology; and so the question becomes one of the role of substance in being. Already, though, the answer is patent on a common-sense basis. Surely, nothing can be or exist, save it be either a substance itself, or else in or of a substance. What else, after all, is the import of the doctrine of the categories, or of the many illustrations and examples of that doctrine that we have already considered? Thus there is no way that a color can be, or a length, or an action, unless it be the color or the length or the action of something—of a substance. The very being of the so-called accidents—of things like colors, sizes, shapes, actions, passions, relations, etc.—is simply to be in or of substances. And as for substances, their being in turn may best be understood negatively or by contrast: for as accidents are the sorts of things that can only be or exist in another (that is, in a substance), so substances, rather than having the sort of dependent being or existence that accidents have, are to be reckoned as being in this sense independent. Their being is not to be in another, but rather to be just in themselves. Or to cap this contrast in the language that has become current among English translators of Aristotle: for an accident to be or to exist it must necessarily be "present in" another, namely, in a substance, but a substance is the sort of thing that does not have to be present in another in order to be or to exist; rather it is or exists as being simply in itself.

Thus if we were for a moment to take but a brief backward glance at those other alternative ontologies which we mentioned earlier in passing, it would seem that the atomists do indeed ascribe to their ultimate atoms a being not altogether unlike that of Aristotelian substances. On the other hand, Aristotle's own account of the being of substances is such as hardly to warrant the restriction of the sorts of things which he calls substances merely to atoms alone; in fact, on other grounds Aristotle would deny that his substances are ever thus atomic in character. What's more, the atomists—at least to judge from the admittedly rather paltry account which we gave of them—seem to make no provision at all for the being of the sorts of things which Aristotle calls accidents.

On the other hand, one might wonder whether Plato's notion of the many changing particulars as somehow participating in, or deriving their being from, the being of the Forms, may not be at least vaguely akin to Aristotle's notion of the being of accidents as somehow present in substances. Yet it is immediately obvious that although the being which Plato's forms have is in a way not unlike the being of Aristotelian substances in that neither the one nor the other is present in anything else,[8] there is at the same time a most palpable difference between the two. For Plato's Forms—such things as triangularity, justice, man's nature as such—are what philosophers are wont to call universals, for the very reason that any number of particulars (that is, individual concrete things) can participate in them. In contrast, Aristotle's substances are not universals but particulars, so that in the language of Aristotle's logic these primary substances must always function as subjects and never as predicates—they cannot be predicated of anything else any more than they can be present in anything else.

Putting aside for the moment any further contrasts of Aristotle's ontology with other ontologies, let us pursue directly the further details of Aristotle's own ontology. Indeed, it might be well if we were to scrutinize, as well as elaborate upon, Aristotle's own contrast of the being of things that exist in themselves (substances) and the being of things that have to exist in another (accidents). Apparently both of these are ways of being, and, to judge from our initial account, accidents are no less beings than substances. But are they? Or rather to approach the same question from a rather different angle: how can accidents no less than substances be said to be beings; or exactly what is that common meaning or sense of *being* that permits one to say of both accidents and substances that they are beings?

A Key Device of Aristotle's Ontology

To this latter question, Aristotle gives a rather subtle, if seemingly a rather initially baffling, answer. *Being,* he says, does not have a common or univocal meaning at all. Hence one cannot properly say that accidents are or exist or have being in the same sense as substances, for there just is no sameness of sense here. But then is the term *being* wholly equivocal or ambiguous, so that when we call substances and accidents both *beings,* we no more mean the same by that term than we do when we call both the side of a river and a financial institution a *bank*? To this, though, Aristotle's response would be No, *being* is not a wholly equivocal term in the way in which *bank* is; rather the meaning of a term like *being* is somehow in between being either wholly equivocal or wholly univocal. How can this be?

To this challenge Aristotle would respond by citing an example. Take a notion like that of *healthy,* he would suggest. May we not say of a person or an animal that he is healthy; and no less of someone's complexion that it is a healthy complexion; or again of a climate that it is healthy? Yet surely an animal, a climate, and a complexion are very different things, radically different in fact. How, then, can they all be equally subsumed under the one notion of being healthy? In other words, in the case of a notion like that of *health*, one has a term or a concept that is neither wholly univocal nor wholly equivocal. Thus health, or the condition of being healthy, applies properly only to animals. Nevertheless, we may properly and not altogether equivocally speak of a climate as being healthy, not, indeed, in the same way that an animal is said to be healthy, but rather in the sense of its being a *cause* or source of health in animals. Or again, a complexion is said to be healthy in the sense of a *sign* of health in a person or an animal. Thus Aristotle would say that a term like *health* or *healthy* is indeed a partially equivocal term, and yet it is equivocal in a very peculiar, and distinctive way: it is the kind of equivocal term that Aristotelian scholars have come to call a "πρὸς ἕν equivocal";[9] that is, although in its different applications a term like *healthy* has quite different meanings, nevertheless these different meanings are all referred to one basic and proper meaning—in this case health as it is in plants or animals—so that it is with reference to this one basic meaning that all sorts of other things besides animals may be said to be "healthy."

Returning, then, to the term *being*, Aristotle considers it to be a πρὸς ἕν equivocal, in the sense that all of the various accidents may be said to be or to have being inasmuch as the being which any and all of them have must be referred to, or understood with reference to, the basic or proper being of substance.

There are many senses in which a thing may be said to "be," but all that "is" is related to one central point, one definite kind of thing, and is not said to "be" by a mere ambiguity. Everything which is healthy is related to health, one thing in the sense that it preserves health, another in the sense that it produces it, another in the sense that it is a symptom of health, another because it is capable of it. And that which is medical is relative to the medical art, one thing being called medical because it possesses it, another because it is naturally adapted to it, another because it is a function of the medical art. And we shall find other words used similarly to these. So, too, there are many senses in which a thing is said to be, but all refer to one starting point; some things are said to be because they are substances, others because they are a process towards substance, or destructions or privations or qualities of substance, or productive or generative of substance, or of things which are relative to substance, or negations of one of these things, or of substance itself. It is for this reason that we say even of non-being that it *is* non-being. As, then, there is one science which deals with all healthy things, the same applies in the other cases also. For not only in the case of things, which have one common notion does the investigation belong to one science, but also in the case of things that are related to one common nature; for even these in a sense have one common notion. It is clear, then, that it is the work of one science also to study the things that are, *qua* being. —But everywhere science deals with that which is primary, and on which the other things depend, and in virtue of which they get their names. If, then, this is substance, it will be of substances that the philosopher must grasp the principles and causes.[10]

The Details of Aristotle's Ontology:
The Being of Forms and of Matter

Aristotle's ontology does not stop merely with this exhibition of what might be called the ontological priority of substance. Directly within substances themselves there is an analogous priority or *pros hen* equivocation, with respect to the being of such elements and principles of substance as are requisite for the being of these same substances. Indeed, it would certainly appear initially plausible that as one may ask on a very general level what it is that is requisite for something to be and answer that it must either be a substance or at least be present in a substance, so also one may ask more specifically what it is that is needed or requisite in order that substances themselves should be. After all, such substances as we are familiar with in our everyday existence—dogs, bushes, rocks, apples, and Chinese—all manifest an undeniable ontological complexity or structure: they not only are, but they are what they are; they exist as individuals, but always as individuals of certain determinate kinds. This intrinsic complexity of ordinary everyday physical substances Aristotle marks by his distinction between the matter and the substantial form of any such substance. Thus already in the context of Aristotle's physics, we have seen how substances must be material, since only through having matter as one of their intrinsic principles are substances able to change. Likewise, in a more properly logical context, Aristotle always insists that primary substances are things such as are always subjects and never predicates. Yet looked at in one way any substantial form—the form or determining principle in virtue of which any substance is the kind of substance it is—a dog a dog, a bush a bush, or a Chinese a Chinese—any such form is of course predicable of any and all the individuals that are characterized by that form; of any individual man we can say that he is a man, of any individual dog that he is a dog, or any bush that it is a bush, etc. Accordingly, if so-called primary substances—substances in their primary and basic sense— can never function as the predicates of subjects in logical propositions, it can only be because such primary substances have a material as well as a formal element or component, which thus renders them particular and individual and so impredicable.[11]

If the real existing substances of the physical world are thus composite of matter and form, then that celebrated question of his *Metaphysics* which we found Aristotle to be asking begins to hint at its own answer: "And indeed the question which was raised of old and is raised now and always, and is always the subject of doubt, namely, what being is, is just the question, what is substance?" [12] Apparently, as the question "What is being?" was to be answered, "It is substance," so now the question "What is substance?" will have to be answered, "Substance is perhaps matter, or maybe it is form, or possibly it is the composite of the two."

Forced to choose between these alternatives as to what substance is—and so ultimately as to what being is as well—Aristotle responds decisively by saying that certainly substance (and likewise being) cannot be understood as simply matter. For the undeniable marks of substance are (1) that substance must be the sort of thing that enjoys a separate and independent existence (it is not the sort of thing that can only exist as present in or dependent on another in the manner of the so-called accidents of substance) and (2) that substance must be something individual and particular, and not anything universal in the manner of Platonic forms.[13] Clearly it is impossible that matter could ever be substance in this sense (or that substance could ever be simply matter). For matter is no more than a mere capacity or potentiality to be this or that; hence as such it is neither this nor that, nor anything determinate at all. Matter, therefore, considered as something that is actually nothing, only a mere ability to be something or other, hardly qualifies for the independence and individuality which are the requisite marks of substance.

Yet is there not an equal and opposite disability attaching to substantial forms? For although forms do not suffer the indeterminacy of matter, being themselves the very principles of substantial determinacy, must they not be disqualified for the role of substance on the same ground as Plato's Forms: they seem not to be individual beings or entities at all, but rather universals?

Nor does the candidacy of the composite of form and matter seem to be much better off in its bid for the office of substance than were the candidacies of either matter or form. To say that substances—at least physical substances—are only composites of matter and form, while certainly not false, is hardly either satisfactory or definitive, since to try to identify the very substance of the real things and entities of the world with a composite of still more ultimate and basic principles and elements only serves to point to those more ultimate elements as being the ultimate locus where the real being or substance of the thing is to be found.

What, then, is to be done? If the substance, and hence the being of things, is to be understood as being neither their matter, nor their form, nor the composition within them of both matter and form, who or what is left to play the title role of substance or being in Aristotle's ontology? Is there nothing left, and is Aristotle's ontology thus forced to close down before its promised performance can even begin? Happily, it is right at this point that the so-called *pros hen* character of being, and of substance, too, can be invoked to save the day. For much as qualities and quantities, and states or conditions of things, etc., all may properly be said to be, and yet can be said to be only with respect to the basic reference-point of substance, so also matter can be said to be the substance of a thing, and yet clearly it is so only with reference to form. Or indeed, the composite may be said to be the substance, and yet only and always with reference to and by means of that which is most truly the substance, the very heart, the very "guts" of the thing—its substantial nature, its essence, its form, its "what," its very quiddity.

But if Aristotle wishes thus to regard "substance" as being a *pros hen* equivocal, no less than "being," and yet at the same time wishes to make all the various candidates for the role of substance depend upon and derive from form as being what is most truly substantial in any so-called substance, then does he not fall right back into Plato's theory of the Forms? Yet, presumably, it was Aristotle himself who originally and continually and repeatedly refused to cast the Forms in the role of substance, simply because Forms are universal, and one of the criteria of substance is that it must be particular and individual.

Once again, the answer to this difficulty is to be found in that *pros hen* character of Aristotle's notion of substance, which presumably is something quite alien to Plato's Forms. Far from existing apart from the particular concrete changing things of the world, Aristotle's substantial forms or essences are thoroughly implicated in such concrete, changing particulars. In fact, such is precisely the sense of that *pros hen* structure of the substance and being of these particulars: it means that the one ultimate reference-point for the understanding of their being and substance—substance as form or essence—is precisely that, a reference-point in just such a setting or referential scheme. Accordingly, as the independence or the existence in itself of substance, as contrasted with the accidents of substance, must not be taken to mean that substances ever exist all alone and without any accidents at all, so also the ultimate being and substantiality of Aristotle's forms and essences certainly does not mean that these forms ever exist as such and as universal and without being themselves individual, or the forms of individuals.

Aristotle's Metaphysics
as Distinguished from His Ontology

We must let this suffice by way of a brief exposi*.o..* and apologia for Aristotle's ontology. But what now of A. *.otle's* "metaphysics"? We have already been at pains to explain that in the *Metaphysics* Aristotle does address himself to the question of being as such or being *qua* being, in the sense of what it is that is requisite for, or is the principle or source of, anything whatever's being able to be or to exist. In addition, he concerns himself with being *qua* being in the sense of trying to determine that which is most truly being, or that which can lay claim to being in the most perfect sense or to the highest degree. Clearly, though, anything that can claim to be or to have being in this sense can be none other than the sort of being or beings as have traditionally been designated as "god" or "the gods"—beings that are immaterial, immutable, supersensible, imperishable, etc. Accordingly, as we have already remarked, a part of Aristotle's *Metaphysics* is devoted to "theology"—to the science or study of god or the gods.

If a somewhat personal value judgment may be permitted, I am certainly tempted to say that Aristotle's theology is hardly that part of Aristotle's *Metaphysics,* or of his philosophy generally, that deserves the most careful examination and study—and this not because Aristotle's theology is not central and fundamental to his metaphysics, for it is; and not because this part of Aristotle was not taken very seriously by subsequent thinkers in Western philosophy; for, on the contrary, it was precisely Aristotle's theology that had an incalculable influence on the history of Western thought for 1,800 years or so. Rather, the reason is that Aristotle's theology, having had such an impact on subsequent thought, particularly Christian thought, was not surprisingly far outstripped by his successors in the West, particularly during the Middle Ages, in the power and precision of their own development of theology. Accordingly, we may perhaps be forgiven for what will be only the most cursory treatment of such theology as is developed in Aristotle.[14]

Perhaps we should begin with a reminder once again of the distinctive nature and character, as well as of the all-pervasiveness in the physical world, of motion and change as Aristotle understood them. Thus we have already noted how Aristotle considers anything and everything in the physical world to be subject to change—to have a potentiality for becoming other and different. Indeed, to have such a potentiality for change is what it means for something to be a physical or material thing. Any actual change or motion is nothing but an actualizing of a given thing's capacity or potentiality for becoming other or different: it (the change) is thus the actual transition, or the actual being on-the-way, from something's being merely able to be thus and so to its actually being thus and so. For any such passage from potency to act, or for such an actualizing of a thing's potentialities, there is always requisite an agent or an efficient cause. Moreover, this agent or efficient cause of the change must be active, or must exercise its agency, continuously throughout the entire process of the change, it being just such an active agency, operating continuously throughout the process, that actually effects the actualization of the potency or the actual transition from potency to act.

Be it noted, however, that, as Aristotle sees it, not only are there changes of this sort actually in process and going on over the whole face of nature, but in addition such changes—be they qualitative or quantitative changes, be they changes of place or substantial changes—have always been going on in nature ever and eternally, nature being just that domain or region of being in which all things are essentially subject to change and at least some things are actually in process of change.

Nor could there ever have been a time in which there was nothing changing at all. Aristotle considers that time is inseparable from change, time being the measure of motion in the sense of the "how-fast" or "how-slow" of motion, so that there could no more be a time without change or motion than there could be a size or a shape without a something that has such size and shape.

Still more to the point is Aristotle's contention that an absolute beginning of change or motion is quite inconceivable. For suppose that there were such an absolutely first change, there would, of course, need to be an agent or efficient cause of such a first change, it being impossible for any potency merely to actualize itself. But this agent or efficient cause must have itself been first able to act, and then subsequently to have actually come into action as the active agent of the first change. What this would appear to entail, however, is that before what by hypothesis was to have been the absolutely first change, there must have been a prior change as a result of which the agent or the efficient cause of the supposedly absolutely first change must itself have changed from being merely able to effect a change to being actually effective or efficient of that change. In other words, for any hypothetically first change there must have been a change before it. Hence an absolutely first change is an impossibility.

No sooner, though, does Aristotle thus establish that change itself could have no absolute beginning, but rather that there must always and from all eternity have been changes going on, than he immediately recognizes that there must be another and still further consequence of this first conclusion. For if for every change that occurs there must be an agent or efficient cause; and if that agent or efficient cause in turn must itself have undergone a change from being merely potentially effective or efficient to being actually so, thus presupposing an even prior agent or efficient cause—is it then possible in the situation as so described to suppose that absolutely all agents and efficient causes are to be thought of as being at one time only potentially active and then later actually so? In other words, is it possible to suppose that with respect to any and every agent or efficient cause there must be a transition from potency to act?

To this question Aristotle responds that the answer can only be "No." For if all agents universally are to be thought of as being obliged to pass from potency to act before they can become active or effective, then it is at least conceivable that at some time—given the infinity of temporal duration—no agent would be active anywhere. If no agent is necessarily active or efficient as such and of itself, but is always dependent upon some prior or outside agent to activate it, then there is nothing self-contradictory in the supposition that such an agent might never be activated, or even that any agent at all should thus ever be activated. But if it is thus conceivable that there might be no agency or efficiency operative anywhere, it is then no less conceivable that there might be no motion or change at all, all change being dependent upon the continuing, concurrent agency of the efficient cause of that change.

However, earlier we saw how Aristotle had shown, presumably successfully, that change could not be other than eternal, and that there simply could not be such a thing as an absolute beginning or end of change. Accordingly, if there must always have been change, there must always have been agencies or efficient causes requisite for the effecting of these changes. Hence it cannot be supposed that the potentialities of agents necessary to effect changes might conceivably none of them be actualized. And so Aristotle concludes that there must be some agents, or at least some one agent, which is necessarily active, or, as Aristotle would put it, is nothing but pure act—that is, which is completely free from all potentiality, and which therefore is in no wise dependent upon any outside agent to bring it from potency to act. Such an agent, therefore, which would be pure act, and which as such would be completely independent of any and every outside agency for its own agency and effectiveness—this agent is just such a being as Aristotle calls god or a god.

What more might one be able to say of the nature of such a so-called divine being, other than that it is pure act? Aristotle's answer is that being thus pure act and hence as lacking any and all potentiality, such a being must needs be immaterial. For Aristotle matter simply means potentiality, and to say that something is material is to say that it is changeable—is potentially other than what it is, either in respect to its quantity or its quality or its place, or even in respect to its very substance. Already, however, we have seen in connection with Aristotle's psychology and with his general account of human beings and of human nature, that anything that is in the nature of intelligence or understanding or mind must be immaterial, and that for the very reason that any act of cognition or of knowing requires that the forms or features of things that come to be known be immaterially received in the knower. Accordingly, given this correlation of intelligence with immateriality, and given that anything that is simply pure act and hence completely lacking in potentiality of any kind must of course be immaterial as well, Aristotle concludes that god or divine being cannot be other than an intelligence: it is pure act or activity, and its action or activity simply the act of thinking or knowing.

What is it, though, that a god so conceived as the continuous and unceasing act of thinking or knowing will think or think about? Aristotle's answer is that any object of divine thought or contemplation could hardly be anything other than god himself, for then the divine thought would be dependent upon a principle outside itself, and as thus dependent upon an outside principle the act of thinking of such a being would no longer be a pure act, but rather the act of a being whose potentialities had been actualized in virtue of some outside principle. Besides, the thinking of a being that was pure act could not undergo any change, since all change is a manifestation of potentiality; accordingly, the pure act of thinking of a divine being could not be directed toward anything that was beneath or inferior to the divine, anything of that sort being necessarily afflicted with potentiality and hence subject to change. So there remains no other object of divine thought than the divine itself, with the result that there emerges that celebrated, not to say rather paradoxical sounding, formula of Aristotle's to the effect that god's thinking is precisely a thinking which, being a thinking of or about itself, is simply a thinking of thinking (ἡ νόησις νοήσεως νόησις).[15]

But Why an Aristotelian Metaphysics at All?

Doubtless, this highly abbreviated account of Aristotle's metaphysics, as over against his ontology, may have impressed the reader only with the seeming implausibility of such metaphysics conceived of as a theology. Be assured, however, that any such implausibility is the fault of our exposition rather than of Aristotle's own doctrines. Still, on one count at least it might well appear that it is not merely an inadequacy in exposition that tends to render this particular phase of the enterprise of Aristotle's metaphysics implausible, as much as the very nature of that enterprise itself. For why a metaphysics in this sense at all? And why not suppose that ontology alone suffices? Why push on, in other words, into the patently dubious domain of a supposed science of metaphysics in the sense of a theology?

This, it will be recalled, is a question which we raised earlier in regard to Aristotle's general project for a *Metaphysics* or First Philosophy, as he called it; and it is a question that now returns to plague us with a new urgency that no longer permits postponement. For it is one thing to say that physics in Aristotle's sense (or in the modern scientific sense as well, for that matter) is not enough, and that there must also be a metaphysics, in the sense of an investigation of what it takes for things to be, or of what is requisite for their very being, considered as such. But this quest after the principles or elements that things must have in order for them to qualify simply as beings or as real beings, is precisely the business of that part or branch of metaphysics that nowadays tends to be called ontology. But why in addition to an ontology in this sense does one also need a theology? In short, it is quite another thing to insist that physics is not enough, in that not only does one need to go beyond physics to metaphysics in the sense of ontology, but one also needs a metaphysics in the sense of a theology.

Moreover, it is right at this point that any number of modern metaphysicians would part company with Aristotle. For while there are not a few distinguished contemporary philosophers—Russell, Sartre, and Bergmann, to mention only three—who would certainly acknowledge the legitimacy of the entire enterprise of ontology, they would steadfastly repudiate any such thing as metaphysics in the sense of theology. It is not difficult to see what their reasons might be. Even with respect to Aristotle, these thinkers would no doubt say that although Aristotle's ontological questions having to do with the necessary dependence in being of accidents upon substances, or having to do with whether for a thing to be or to exist principles like form and matter or act and potency are requisite—although these, indeed, are not questions that are resolvable by ordinary scientific procedures of empirical verification and falsification, they are nevertheless questions that bear directly upon things and events in the natural world and hence upon things and events that in no wise transcend our human experience. And in this sense and for this very reason these same contemporary thinkers would undoubtedly acknowledge that such Aristotelian ontological questions are entirely legitimate as issues and questions in philosophy. But when it comes to metaphysical questions as to the being and nature of god, or more generally as to the being and nature of causes and entities outside the physical universe altogether—such questions our contemporary philosophers, even those of them who are admittedly ontologists, would say are spurious and improper.

Yet note in passing what a serious sacrifice this anti-metaphysical stance imposes upon its holders. Consider Gustav Bergmann, for example. Following Russell's tradition of so-called "logical atomism," Bergmann wishes, through a process of logical analysis of what is presented to us in sensory experience, to be able to reach those irreducible ontological elements out of which everything else in the actual world of our human experience may be seen to be built up and compounded. Moreover, since our everyday sensory experience seems, at least on one very plausible line of analysis, to be built up out of various minimal sensory data—colored shapes, sounds of various kinds, odors, tactile qualities, etc.—Bergmann proceeds to analyze these rudimentary data in order to try to determine what their ontological structure and character must be, or what it is about them that enables them to be, or that fits them out as beings. As a result of his analyses, Bergmann concludes that any such sensory datum—say, a tiny red patch of color—must comprise at once a particular and a universal. Thus the patch of red is perforce *this* patch, and hence particular; and at the same time it is a patch of red, of a certain size and shape, and perhaps with other features as well—all universals. Accordingly, Bergmann concludes that the ultimate ontological entities—or, as Russell would say, "the ultimate furniture of the world"—are simply particulars and universals. It is these that are the atoms or ontological building-blocks out of which everything else is made; likewise, it is through these and with respect to these that one can say of any and all real facts in the world that ultimately these facts may be seen to involve the simple ontological structure of particulars exemplifying universals.

Or take Sartre. In his ontology he simply posits what we might call two ultimates, Being on the one hand, or the in-itself, and Consciousness, or the for-itself, on the other. As to Being, it is just that—sheer undifferentiated, unqualified, characterless, meaningless being. In contrast, Consciousness is a negating of being, a distancing of itself from being, a "taking" of being in various ways, so that in consequence of how we take or interpret being there emerges for us our own actually lived world, a structured, articulated, and valued world of changing things and persons and events. In other words, for Sartre no less than for Bergmann—as for Aristotle too in his way—ontology is the determining of those ultimate entities or principles that are essential and requisite for the make-up and constitution of what might be called the realities of our everyday experience. For Aristotle, these ultimates are substances and their accidents, or perhaps form and matter; for Bergmann they are particulars and universals; for Sartre they are the In-itself and the For-itself.

Nevertheless, the question before us is why it should ever be supposed—as Aristotle does indeed suppose—that in addition to such ontological ultimates as are embedded right in the realities of our everyday experience, we also need to go further and infer the existence of transcendent entities that lie completely outside the physical or sensible world altogether, and that can no longer be considered to be embedded directly in the facts before us, and whose only reason for being is that they supposedly provide a completely transcendent, or transempirical, or, if you will, meta-physical grounding even for those ontological ultimates that we have acknowledged to be requisite for and constitutive of the everyday sensible and physical realities with which we are all familiar. Surely, however, the answer to this question lies ready to hand.

Consider for a moment Bergmann's ontological ultimates, or Sartre's. Why should the nature of things be so ordered as to make particulars and universals, or, quite differently, Being and Consciousness, requisite as ontological ultimates? Indeed, suppose that in truth it is Bergmann who is right as against Sartre, and that the ontological ultimates of our world are, in fact, particulars and universals. Is it not at least conceivable that things might have been ordered otherwise? After all, Sartre with his rival ontology holds that they are ordered otherwise. Yet even assuming Bergmann's ontology to be correct, all this means is that the ontological hypothesis of particulars and universals is a better and more adequate hypothesis than that of Being and Consciousness. Still, there is nothing about the mere notion of a particular or of a universal, in Bergmann's sense, to indicate that such entities are altogether free from potentiality. Quite the contrary, that they should be the actual ultimate entities, rather than some others—say Sartre's, or even Aristotle's—points to the radical contingency of these entities: they are in fact the ultimates, but it is conceivable that another and entirely different set of entities might have been the actual ontological ultimates instead. In other words, considered as such and in itself, Bergmann's scheme of particulars and universals is only a scheme of possible or potential ultimates. If even in fact these are the ultimates, they are so in virtue of their possibility or their potentiality having been actualized.

No sooner, though, is this much conceded, than Aristotle's decisively metaphysical, as contrasted with any mere ontological, principle becomes operative—the principle, namely, that act or actuality must always be prior to potentiality. Nor does this principle come down to anything more than the simple truth that potencies don't actualize themselves: no matter how flammable a substance is, something must happen to ignite it if it is actually to burn; otherwise, it will for all eternity remain simply able to burn without ever actually burning. So it is that Aristotle's concern to find some agent or some principle of actuality sufficient to account ultimately and finally for the actualization of the potentialities of things in the world led him to infer the existence of something outside of and beyond the world altogether, namely, a god who is sheer agency or actuality without any potentiality at all.

When many of our contemporary philosophers, for all of their partiality to metaphysics in the sense of ontology, nevertheless refuse to go "beyond physics" in the search of the metaphysical in the sense of that which is pure act and not potential at all, these same philosophers give every appearance of stopping short of metaphysics by simply not facing up to the issue. Having posited their ontological ultimates as if they were necessary hypotheses for accounting for the realities of the everyday sensible world, these latter-day metaphysicians then seem blithely to ignore the fact that even if certain hypothetical entities may be considered to have been adequately established in virtue of their explanatory value, the question is still left open as to what the actual causes must be of these same hypothetical entities, which, even though they may well be actual, nevertheless require that such an actualization of their own intrinsic potentiality be accounted for in terms of the prior actuality of their causes.[16]

What if Aristotle's Metaphysics Should Prove to Be Double-Visioned?

Alas, we are still not done with the issues which Aristotle's *Metaphysics* has raised and continues to raise, both in present-day philosophy and in the whole history of philosophy. For that matter, even if the apologia which we mounted on behalf of Aristotle in the foregoing section were to be pronounced successful, and if it were accordingly to appear justified at least to some that Aristotle should so extend the domain of metaphysics as to make it include a theology, the very warrant which would thus be extended to

Aristotle to incorporate a theology right within his metaphysics would, on other grounds, seem seriously to compromise Aristotle's own expressed statements as to what metaphysics or first philosophy is and what it is all about. Have we not already noted how metaphysics for Aristotle is supposed to be concerned simply with being *qua* being, or with being as such? We have also seen how Aristotle himself intended that such an account of the subject matter of metaphysics should be construed. The very thing that distinguishes the other sciences—for example, physics and mathematics—from metaphysics, he notes, is that each of the former disciplines separates off one portion or kind of being and investigates it, whereas metaphysics investigates being in general, or, if you prefer, what it is that is requisite for anything whatever simply to be, as against what might be requisite for it to be in process of change or to be in the manner of mathematical entities, etc. What, then, is one to make of what would now seem to be a new dimension or emphasis in Aristotle's metaphysics—that metaphysics, far from being concerned with any and all being, with being *qua* being, is rather concerned with a particular kind of being, that is, with god, or with divine being or perfect being?

Surely, this seems to betoken a serious and radical inconsistency right within Aristotle's own concept or understanding of what his metaphysics or first philosophy is all about. For one simply cannot hold that metaphysics is concerned simply with what it takes for a thing—anything and everything—to be, and then turn around and say that metaphysics is concerned precisely with what it takes for the most perfect of all beings, god or the pure act of thought, to be. In fact, so profoundly has this issue agitated philosophers, and more particularly classical scholars of the nineteenth century and after, that the most incredible theories and explanations have been put forward to account for this seeming radical inconsistency in Aristotle's metaphysics. Some men of rather more scholarly arrogance and recklessness than others have announced that it is simply inconceivable that the great Aristotle should ever have been guilty of such an inconsistency, with the result that they have proceeded rather high-handedly to decree that all of the texts in which Aristotle speaks of god and of theology are spurious and must therefore be excised from the Aristotelian corpus. Others, men with less liking for Aristotle and with more textual caution, have taken the line, sometimes with ill-concealed glee, that Aristotle is not to be taken seriously after all; he flatly contradicts himself, and the texts prove it. Still others have apparently been so smitten with their veneration for Aristotle that they would spare their master even to the point of making a virtue of muddleheadedness. Aristotle was a thinker of such rare honesty, they seem to be saying, that in his troubled searching for the truth he gropes and fumbles about, now saying one thing and now almost the direct opposite, and yet always ingenuously and with no effort at concealment at all. Still another reaction to the seeming inconsistency in Aristotle's project for his metaphysics has been to follow at once a more judicious and more ingenious line—it consists of falling back on the notion of an historical evolution in Aristotle's thought to explain the seeming inconsistency. Thus, why might it not be that when Aristotle was younger and more starry-eyed and fresh from the influence of Plato, he was naturally inclined to romance about god and things divine? But given increased age and, if not increased wisdom then perhaps increased intellectual sobriety, Aristotle may very naturally have fallen into more "scientific" and less speculative interests and habits of thought: rather than trying to rise to the heights in search of god, he would occupy himself instead with more mundane things like being itself, any being, and not necessarily the being of god at all. And so by this last account there is not so much contradiction in Aristotle as development: in youth he may have occupied himself with god, but no sooner had he come to man's estate, than he put aside childish things, and instead of aspiring to be a theologian was content to be only an ontologist.[17]

Happily, however, it would seem that for our part we may simply put to one side all of these impressive and incredible exertions, particularly of the classical scholars, with respect to the seeming contradiction in Aristotle's metaphysics. For it could well be that there simply is no contradiction in the first place; or at least there ought not to be any, once one reminds oneself of how careful Aristotle is ever to insist that the subject matter of metaphysics must always be understood in terms of *pros hen* equivocation.

Thus in saying that metaphysics is concerned simply with being and with what it means for things to be, he does not intend that his readers should consider *being* to have but a single sense or meaning, or should take being itself to be merely one single sort of thing. Quite the contrary. No sooner does he say that the subject matter of metaphysics is being, than, as we have already seen, he immediately presses on to say that this implies that the true subject matter of metaphysics is really substance. Not that there are no beings other than substances. Far from it, for accidents are as undeniably beings as are substances; and yet the being of any accident must always be referred to and can only be understood in reference to substance.

So also as regards form and matter. For as the beings of things other than substance must be referred to the being of substance, so the being of any substance needs to be understood as the being of the substantial form or essence of that substance. Nor is this to say that matter, as contrasted with form, has no being at all; rather it is to say that the being of matter and the being of forms have both to be understood in terms of *pros hen* equivocation: matter, that is to say, is or has being only with reference to form.

Analogously, we can now begin to see how Aristotle's theology, in turn, is entirely reconcilable with his ontology in terms of this same sort of *pros hen* equivocation. For why should not a concern with being *qua* being be understood as a concern with being in the truest or most perfect sense? Not that nothing other than that which is pure act is even being at all. On the contrary. All those beings that are permeated and shot through with potentiality are of course being. Yet, clearly, actuality is prior to potentiality: that is to say, the potential can only be and be understood with reference to the actual; or to put the same thing in other terms, the being of all things other than god can only be and be understood with reference to god.

But let Aristotle make the point in his own words:

> One might raise the question whether first philosophy is in any way universal or is concerned merely with some genus and some one nature. In the case of the mathematical sciences, their objects are not all treated in the same manner; geometry and astronomy are concerned with some nature, but universal mathematics is common to all. Accordingly, if there were no substances other than those formed by nature, physics would be the first science; but if there is an immovable substance, this would be prior, and the science of it would be first philosophy *and would be universal in this manner, in view of the fact that it is first.* And it would be the concern of this science, too, to investigate being *qua* being, both what being is and what belongs to it *qua* being.[18]

Surely, the question of the unity of subject matter in Aristotle's *Metaphysics* hardly seems to warrant the great difficulty that has been made of it. Far from Aristotle's own characterization of that subject matter being either inconsistent or self-contradictory, the whole issue would appear to be if not much ado about nothing, then surely much ado about very little. Enough said.

Chapter VI

Last But Not Least, Logic

It may seem to many as if we had got the cart before the horse, having talked about Aristotle for some five chapters and only now, in the concluding chapter, turning our attention to Aristotle's logic. For centuries the tradition has been always to approach the study of Aristotle, whether in manuals, or text-books, or other expositions of Aristotle's philosophy, by giving a certain pride of place to the logic, as if it belonged at the beginning and in the very first chapter. Aristotle himself leaves no doubt that in his eyes you cannot properly, in one and the same investigation, concern yourself both with the subject matter under investigation and with an investigation as to what tools and methods might be requisite for any investigation of any subject matter whatever. Accordingly, those of Aristotle's writings that were classified under the title of the *Organon*—signifying, simply, the instrument of knowledge or of scientific investigation—ought in principle to be mastered first, before one goes on to the study of *Physics, Psychology, Metaphysics, Ethics,* and the rest.

All the same, one cannot overlook the fact that, like the old gray mare, Aristotle's logic just ain't what it used to be! Until the turn of this century, the intellectual community in general, to say nothing of philosophers in particular, seem never to have doubted that Aristotle's logic was practically equivalent to logic itself. Thus Kant, who was certainly not given to indiscriminate praise of his predecessors, puts it forth as being a thing almost beyond discussion:

> That logic has already, from the earliest times, proceeded upon this sure path is evidenced by the fact that since Aristotle it has not required to retrace a single step, unless, indeed, we care to count as improvements the removal of certain needless subtleties or the clearer exposition of its recognized teaching, features which concern the elegance rather than the certainty of the science. It is remarkable also that to the present day this logic has not been able to advance a single step, and is thus to all appearance a closed and completed body of doctrine.[1]

· But things are different nowadays. It is as if the roof had fallen in on Aristotelian logic only within the last fifty to seventy-five years. True, modern logicians do not necessarily say that as a result of this great revolution, Aristotle's logic has been shown to be altogether wrongheaded or mistaken. Rather they would say that that logic has been shown to be but a minor and comparatively insignificant part of the overall discipline of logic, or of mathematics and logic taken together. In fact, an analogy here with Ptolemaic astronomy might be somewhat apt: for as one might say that Ptolemaic astronomy has not been shown to be absolutely false or wrongheaded, it being still entirely adequate for certain limited purposes and within a limited context—say, that of navigation in the Mediterranean—so also Aristotelian logic is a not unreliable guide in certain limited types of inference and everyday arguments, but within the larger context of purely formal mathematico-logical systems in general, Aristotelian logic is hopelessly outmoded and inadequate.

Such at least is the fashionable contemporary view of Aristotelian logic. But despite its current fashion, to say nothing of the weight of contemporary authority behind it, we would venture to say that such a view is misleading, if not outright mistaken. What would appear to have happened is that most modern logicians and philosophers have tended pretty much to forget the distinctive kind of instrument that Aristotle's logic was supposed to be, as well as what it was supposed to be an instrument for. Instead, having made a number of assumptions of their own as to exactly what logic might be and what it might be for, they then found it easy to condemn Aristotelian logic as scarcely meeting these somewhat factitious standards which they themselves had set up.

To offer but a foretaste of the sort of rebuttal that we shall presently try to develop in more detail, it is significant that Aristotle's logic was something which he considered to be a proper organon—that is, a proper device or tool or method—for achieving a knowledge of the sort that is exhibited in Aristotelian philosophy as a whole; in the *Physics* or the *Metaphysics,* for example. In contrast, modern logicians, insofar as they might be inclined to think of logic as being an organon of knowledge at all, would not surprisingly tend to identify such knowledge with scientific knowledge in the modern sense. Yet clearly Aristotle's physics and modern physics may both of them be called *physics* only in virtue of a serious equivocation in the meaning of the term. Nor would it be in the least surprising that the sort of logic that might serve as an instrument for the attainment of the one type of knowledge could hardly function as a proper instrument in the attainment of another and radically different type of knowledge. Accordingly, suppose that it be granted, at least for purposes of argument, that a physical and metaphysical knowledge of a roughly Aristotelian sort is a perfectly valid and proper knowledge in its own right, which complements, rather than is displaced by, the sort of knowledge that is attainable by sciences in the modern sense. Would not one then be more ready to acknowledge that a logic that was instrumental to the one type of knowledge could hardly be dismissed in favor of another and rather different logic that was instrumental to another and very different type of knowledge?

With this, our reasons may begin to come clear for reversing the normal order and for treating Aristotle's logic at the end rather than at the beginning. Although such a logic is, indeed, but a propaedeutic to Aristotelian philosophy as a whole, it becomes difficult, given the competing logics of the present day, to appreciate such a logic as being such a propaedeutic unless one considers it precisely against the background, rather than simply in the foreground, of Aristotle's philosophy taken in its totality.

Aristotelian Logic as Simply a Device for Knowing What Things Are and Why They Are

To the question, then: How does Aristotle conceive of logic as something that provides the way and the means to knowledge such as he understood it to be—that is, to physical knowledge and to metaphysical knowledge, and even to practical and productive knowledge in an Aristotelian sense? Answering in a single sentence, one might say that Aristotle thought of logic as being just the tool through which we come to know and understand things for what they are and why they are. In short, it is the natures of things and the causes of things that are the key to our understanding of things, and it is the purpose of logic to mediate such a knowledge of the *what*'s and the *why*'s of things.

Thus practically at the outset of our discussion of Aristotle's philosophy we noticed how basic to everything else was Aristotle's doctrine of the categories. The reason was that in the sort of common-sense approach to things that Aristotle follows, if one wants to know what anything is—be it a fish or a plant, a length of something or an action, a location of something or the relation of one thing to another—in any and all such cases what the thing one is considering must ultimately be recognized as being is either a substance or a quantity or a doing of something or a place or a relation, or what not. In other words, the categories as a basic classification of the ultimate kinds of entities is also a classification of the *what*'s of things. And then, making an immediate transition from physics or ontology to language or logic, is it not obvious that as what things are are either substances or quantities or actions or relations, so also to say or to think what anything is we must use as our ultimate descriptive predicates such notions as substance and quantity and relation and place, etc.? In fact, Aristotle's very word *category* can be taken to mean in Greek simply a predicate or a way of thinking or characterizing or describing a thing for what it is.

Accordingly, no less than the cornerstone of Aristotle's logic is what has often been called the S-P or subject-predicate proposition. To take an obvious example, in the statement "Fido is a dog," the subject term in the statement, *Fido,* stands for the particular thing that on the occasion of making that statement one is talking about, namely, Fido; and the predicate term or concept, *dog,* signifies what one takes that subject to be, namely, a dog. Looked at in this way, a so-called subject-predicate proposition may be seen to be an instrument or device for saying or thinking what something is, the subject term standing simply for that which we happen to be talking about or want to know about, and the predicate standing for what we take that thing to be.

Or to vary our example a bit, suppose that instead of "Fido is a dog," we say "A dog is an animal," and perhaps add, "An animal is a substance." Notice that in all three of these examples the predicate simply indicates what the subject—*Fido, dog, animal*—in each case is: a dog, an animal, a substance. Moreover, taking these three particular examples together, or cumulatively, one can see how the ontological doctrine of the categories is directly pertinent here to the logical functioning of S-P propositions. For whether it be Fido or dogs or animals that one is talking about, it is obvious that all of them are ultimately substances. In contrast, if it were a particular shade of green that one happened to be talking about rather than about Fido or about dogs, one could hardly say that the green was a substance. No, what green is is a color, and what a color is ultimately is a quality. Or if it were a certain distance that one was talking about, say three miles, then what that is would be neither a substance nor a quality, but a quantity. So also for any and everything in any and all of the other categories as well.

Through such rough and ready examples as these we can perhaps get at least an inkling of how Aristotelian subject-predicate propositions are supposed to function as instruments through which we come to recognize things for what they are. But the story is still not complete. Suppose that instead of saying "Fido is a dog," we were to say something like "Fido is in the kennel," or "Fido is running," or "Fido is the sire of Boots." Clearly, in each of the latter cases we would again have a subject-predicate proposition, the subject signifying what we were talking about and the predicate what we were saying about it, or predicating of it.[2] At the same time, could it be said that this time the predicate terms signify what the subject is? Apparently not, for it is clear that what Fido is is a substance, and not a quality or a quantity or a relation, etc. Yet a predicate such as *in the kennel* would seem to indicate where Fido is, and not what he is; or *running* would appear to signify not what he is but rather what he is doing, just as *being the sire of* indicates his relationship to Boots. Accordingly, these latter predicates are clearly subsumable under the categories of place, action, and relation, and not of substance at all.

Nevertheless, the way this situation is dealt with in Aristotle's logic is by drawing a rather common-sense distinction between different ways in which predicates may be related to their subjects, or different relationships of predicability, as they are called. Thus briefly, some predicates are related to their subjects essentially and others accidentally. For example, in Fido's case what he is essentially is a dog, an animal, a substance. Moreover, being a substance of a particular kind, rather than being a mere quantity or relation or place, is just what is of the very nature or essence of Fido. Clearly, though, what Fido is essentially is not the only thing or things that may be said of him. For Fido can perfectly well be of a certain size, or in a certain place, or doing certain things, etc. Indeed, as we have already seen in discussing Aristotle's physics and ontology, so-called accidents are the sorts of things that must and do exist in or of substances. Transposing this feature of Aristotle's ontology to a logical context, we find that in language and logic, as we can say what something is essentially, so also we can equally well say what it is accidentally: Fido, for example, in addition to being a substance, may also be in a certain place (in the kennel), may be doing various things (running), may be related to various other things (being the sire of Boots), etc.

The Syllogism as an Instrument
for Knowing Causes

Letting this, then, suffice at least for the moment by way of indicating how the subject-predicate propositions of Aristotelian logic function as instruments for our knowing things in terms of what they are, it is high time that we had a look at those further instruments through which we come to know things in terms of their causes, or in terms of why they are. This time the relevant instrument is not a single subject-predicate proposition, but rather a particular kind of patterning or grouping of propositions that has come to be known by the famous or infamous name of the *syllogism.* Now to see what sort of a thing a syllogism is, let us again look at a couple of examples of Aristotelian subject-predicate propositions. Suppose that instead of saying "Fido is a dog," or "Fido is running," or "Dogs are animals," we were to say "Dogs bark," meaning that this was somehow a distinguishing feature, all things being equal, of any and all dogs. Would such a proposition as this purport to be telling us what dogs are essentially, in the same manner as, say, a proposition like "Dogs are animals"? Somehow, it would seem that the answer to such a question could hardly be "Yes," at least not unequivocally. For even if it were to be thought that any and all dogs are necessarily given to barking and that they do so in virtue of their very nature or essence as dogs, still one cannot help noticing that ultimately what dogs are essentially are animals of a certain kind, and ultimately substances of a certain kind. But to say that dogs bark is not in this sense to say what dogs are, but rather what they do. And barking is certainly not classifiable as a substance at all; if anything, it would seem to be classifiable as a kind of action.

Nor is this in the least surprising, for recalling our earlier account of Aristotle's doctrine of the categories, it is a matter of simple common sense that substances in Aristotle's sense should have all sorts of accidents pertaining to them: they are of various sizes (quantity), have various characteristics (quality), are located here or there (place), have things done to them (*passion*), themselves do various things (action), etc. Notice, though, that no sooner do we recognize that substances do indeed have various accidents pertaining to them, than the question immediately becomes pertinent as to why, for example, a certain accident should pertain to a certain substance—what, in other words, are the causes of such a thing? Why do dogs bark; or why does silver melt at

960.5°C, rather than at some other temperature; or why do the angles of a triangle equal two right angles, or why should it be characteristic of human beings that they should use language, etc.? In all of these cases the search for the why or the cause is relevant precisely with respect to the situation of an accident's pertaining to a substance.

Accordingly, taking the barking of dogs as our example, if we ask why dogs bark, we might answer that it is because of certain anatomical features of their heads and throats. Or if we were inclined toward a more teleological answer, we might say that dogs bark in order to frighten suspected enemies, or something of the sort. In any case, whatever be the particular cause, or the particular kind of cause (Aristotle would say that such causes might be either material, formal, efficient, or final causes) that might be adduced to explain why dogs bark, the logical structure of such a causal explanation would have a distinctive common form. Considered formally, to ask for an explanation of something in terms of its cause, is in effect to ask why a certain subject, S, happens to be P, or comes to have P attaching to it as one of its accidents. And the answer to such a question will normally be of the form: S is P, because it is M. In other words, dogs bark, because of the anatomical features of their heads and throats; or the angles of a triangle are equal to two right angles, because each of its angles is equal to one of the three angles around a straight line; or silver melts at the temperature it does because of its particular atomic structure. Moreover, in all of these cases, the answer to the question "Why?" in terms of the relevant cause or causes takes the following form or syllogistic structure:

S is P, because
S is M, and
Any M is P.

Or to use the traditional schema:

$$M \text{ is } P$$
$$S \text{ is } M$$
$$\therefore S \text{ is } P.$$

What is particularly noteworthy about these examples and illustrations is that just as it is evident to us that a why-question must be answered in terms of a certain cause or reason, so is it no less evident that no sooner does one thus attempt to adduce a cause or a reason in answer to a question "Why?," than one finds oneself using a certain standard logical form or pattern—a pattern in which the explanation of why S is P is set forth in terms of a common or mediating term, M, which being connected with both the S and the P terms thus serves quite literally to mediate between them, or, if you will, actually to exhibit, as it were, why S is P.

Now it is true, and Aristotle himself makes much of the fact, that such syllogistic forms or inferences can be considered purely formally. Regardless of what it is that one may be trying to explain through a syllogistic argument, whether it be something about dogs or triangles or chemical elements or whatever, and regardless of what the particular cause or reason may be through which the explanation happens to be made, there are certain invariant syllogistic inference patterns which one must use, and the validity of which can be determined quite independently of the particular content or subject matter of one's argument. For instance, as one invariant form for explaining why S is P is the one cited above—namely, that S is M and M is P—so also one might explain why, in a given case, S is not P on the ground that while any S is M, no M is ever P.

Proceeding, then, in like manner, one can go on to determine all sorts of variant syllogistic forms, together with their relevant properties and characteristics. Nor is it syllogistic arguments alone that are susceptible of this formal treatment. Similarly, S-P propositions can be considered simply in terms of their formal relationships and properties. Thus if S is P, it cannot be non-P; or if no S is P, then no P is S; or if it is false that some S's are not P, then it is true that at least some S's are P, etc. Be it noted, however, that although Aristotle, particularly in the *Prior Analytics*, is most concerned to trace out these purely formal features and relationships of logical propositions and arguments, he is no less concerned, particularly in his *Posterior Analytics*, to remind his students and readers of the point and purpose of these various propositional forms and argument forms so far as knowledge is concerned. For they are, he would insist, instruments through which we seek to determine the *what*'s and the *why*'s of things. In this respect Aristotle's logic is a logic that is presumably rather differently conceived from the sort of thing that goes by the name of logic today.

Induction As Contrasted with Deduction

Before we consider further this contrast of Aristotelian logic with modern logic, there is still another whole side—or perhaps, better, another whole arm—of Aristotle's logic that needs to be considered—inductive logic as over against deductive logic. Indeed, it is easy to see that if logic is to be understood as being no less than the organon of knowledge, then there must certainly be more to it than the mere deductive apparatus of the syllogism. Consider again our trivial example of explaining why dogs bark. Formally considered, the answer to this question as to why S is P had to be in terms of something else that S is, namely, M. However, from our still earlier discussion we learned how all subject-predicate statements are really "what-statements." Whether we be saying that S is P or S is M, we are simply saying what S is, and saying what it is, as we noted earlier, either essentially or accidentally.

Nevertheless, recalling our earlier account of all this, it will be remembered that it was precisely when we asserted what a thing is accidentally rather than essentially, that an explanation seemed called for, or a "why-question" immediately became pertinent. Thus "barking," we noted in the case of our hackneyed example, is not even in the same category as "dog," and it was for the very reason that an action or mode of behavior like barking is not in any sense a substance, as clearly dogs certainly are, that some sort of cause or ground or reason seemed called for as to just why that action should be held to pertain to dogs.

Contrast, though, "Dogs are animals" or "Dogs are substances" with "Dogs bark." With respect to the fact asserted by the latter statement, we can quite properly ask "Why?"—what is the cause of such action or behavior in the case of dogs? But in the case of the two former statements the question "Why?" seems not appropriate at all. "Why is a dog an animal?," or "Why is an animal a substance?" That a dog should be an animal is the sort of thing for which there is no cause, at least not in any proper sense. Rather the most that one could say might be to the effect that being an animal is simply what a dog is, or that that is simply what we mean by the word *dog*. In other words, a why-question simply is not appropriate in such a case.

By way of still further examples, is it not evident that while we can very properly ask why the angles of a triangle are equal to two right angles, we can scarcely ask, at least not with logical or linguistic propriety, why a triangle is a plane figure. Or again, "Why does silver melt at 960.5°C?" seems an entirely proper question, but hardly "Why is silver an element?" In short, what we have called why-questions would clearly seem to be appropriate only with respect to statements that assert what things are accidentally, as over against what they are essentially.

Unfortunately, however, this gives rise to a rather serious problem. For how is it that we come to know what things are essentially, as against what they are only accidentally. With respect to the latter, our knowledge is effected through a knowledge of their causes. Or perhaps we might change our terminology here a bit and say that with respect to accidental predications or what-statements that are only accidental, we can in principle come to know the truth of such statements through a syllogistic demonstration of their causes or reasons. But alas, in the case of essential predications, why-questions are simply impertinent; and hence any sort of deductive or syllogistic demonstration of the truth of such statements through adducing causes and reasons would appear to be quite impossible. All the same, there must be some way in which we come to know what things are essentially. For example, "What is a human being—essentially, that is, and not just accidentally?" or "What is a triangle?" or "What is change or motion?" or "What is being just as such?" or "What is a geological fault?" or "What is cancer?" or "What is happiness, or the good life for man?" These and a thousand and one other questions like them are perfectly legitimate questions. In fact, some of them we can readily recognize as being typically Aristotelian questions. All of them are properly human questions. But if they are questions, then they must be questions the answers to which we do not necessarily know or have not always known; and if they are legitimate questions, then they must be questions that have proper answers. But how may we come by answers to such essential what-questions; what means or methods or instruments may we use to arrive at such answers, particularly if the instrument of deductive syllogistic demonstration is ruled out as impertinent and improper?

Quite apart from the intrinsic legitimacy of such essential

what-questions, there is another reason why it is important to know whether there are means and methods at our disposal for answering questions of this sort and, if so, what they are. As one may have already guessed from our discussion thus far, there is a sense in which even the syllogism as the proper means for our answering why-questions is in most instances dependent ultimately for its cogency upon a prior answer to just such essential what-questions. Consider the matter for a minute purely formally: if S is P in the sense we have been considering—that P signifies what S is not essentially but only accidentally—then a why-question is immediately in order; yet, if we answer the question as to why S is P by saying that it is because S is M, the same question will arise all over again as to why S should be M, supposing, that is, that "S is M" for its part is but an accidental what-statement and not an essential one. With this, however, we would seem to be confronted with the possibility of an infinite regress: S is P, because it is M; and S is M because it is N, and S is N because it is O, and so on *ad infinitum;* at each stage of the explanation the why-question recurs, and apparently so as never to receive a final or ultimate answer. Nor can the regress be stopped until one comes upon a what-statement in regard to S that is essential and not accidental. We have already noted how it is only with respect to statements as to what a thing is essentially, and not just accidentally, that a why-question finally becomes improper or irrelevant.

What is thus suggested by a consideration of the matter purely formally is further borne out and reinforced when we consider what would appear to be demanded by the very nature of the case, no matter what the particular content or subject matter of our explanation and demonstration might happen to be. Given the particular determinate or essential form of anything, be it an oak tree or a hydrogen atom or a triangle or a relation, say, like that of equality, or the unmoved mover, or whatever, will it not follow from the very nature of such a thing that certain properties will pertain to it, or that it will act and react and behave in certain determinate ways. Thus the growth of an oak tree will hardly be like that of a tadpole; or a relation like that of equality will be a transitive relation, whereas that of "father of" is not; or the properties that follow from the nature of a triangle will be quite different from those that are consequent upon the natures of squares or of circles. Accordingly, as we recognize that from the nature or essence of any X certain further properties or characteristic behavior patterns of X will follow, so also, and going at it from the other end, we recognize that given a certain characteristic property of X or behavior pattern of X, we can quite properly ask why X behaves in that way rather than some other, or why this particular property pertains to X rather than some other; and the answer to such why-questions must ultimately be in terms of the nature of X, or of what X is essentially.

With this we are brought back to our questions of a little earlier. How do we come to know what things are essentially? What means and methods do we have for answering such essential what-questions? Aristotle's reply to this is that it is by means of induction that we come by such answers and achieve a knowledge of this particular kind. Deduction, as we have already seen, is simply ruled out as a means of coming to know the *what*'s or essences of things. But what then is induction, and how does it serve to bring about such a knowledge of essences? Perhaps we could do no better here than simply to let Aristotle himself speak on behalf of his own doctrine. How, he asks, do we come by such a knowledge of the very natures and essences of things—a knowledge which is the very basis and presupposition of all our deductive demonstration and explanations? It is hardly to be supposed that a knowledge of this sort is somehow innate in us and simply possessed from birth. Rather, he says, it must be an acquired knowledge. But acquired from what and how? To this his answer is that it is acquired from sense-perception. For it

> is an obvious characteristic of all animals [that] they possess a congenital discriminative capacity which is called sense-perception. But though sense perception is innate in all animals, in some the sense-impression comes to persist, in others it does not. So animals in which this persistence does not come to be have either no knowledge at all outside the act of perceiving, or no knowledge of objects of which no impression persists; animals in which it does come into being have perception and can continue to retain the sense-impression in the soul: and when such persistence is frequently repeated a further distinction at once arises between those which out of persistence of such sense-impressions develop a power of systematizing them and those which do not. So out of sense-perception comes to be what we call memory, and out of frequently repeated memories of the same thing develops experience; for a number of memories constitute a single experience. From experience again—*i.e.,* from the universal now stabilized in its entirety within the soul, the one beside the many which is a single identity within them all—originate the skill of the craftsman and the knowledge of the man of science, skill in the sphere of coming to be and science in the sphere of being.
>
> We conclude that these states of knowledge are neither innate in determinate form, nor developed from other higher states of knowledge but from sense-perception. It is like a rout in battle stopped by first one man making a stand and then another, until the original formation has been restored. The soul is so constituted as to be capable of this process. . . .
>
> When one of a member of logically indiscriminable particulars has made a stand, the earliest universal is present in the soul: for though the act of sense-perception is of the particular, its content is universal—is man, for example, not the man Callias. A fresh stand is made among these rudimentary universals, and the process does not cease until the indivisible concepts, the true universals, are established:

such and such a species of animal is a step toward the genus animal, which by the same process is a step towards a further generalization.

Thus it is clear that we must get to know the primary premisses by induction; for the method by which even sense-perception implants the universal is inductive.[3]

Such, then, is Aristotle's conception of the nature of induction and of its decisive and indispensable role in the attainment of any and all knowledge. For if knowledge ultimately consists simply in our coming to appreciate or recognize facts and things for what they are, then certain guidelines for the attainment of knowledge would thereby appear to be determined by the very nature of the case. For the most part, to be sure, our knowledge is only a knowledge of what things are accidentally; it is—to express it formally and abstractly—but a knowledge of the fact *that* S is P, and yet without our necessarily seeing or understanding *why* it is P. Nor is such a knowledge of the mere fact that S is P ever cogent or conclusive as knowledge until we do indeed come to see why it is so, or what the reason or cause is for S's being P. But such a knowledge of why S is P must ultimately depend on our recognizing what S is essentially; and, as we have seen, a knowledge of such essential *what*'s, or of the very natures or essences of things, is not a knowledge that can in any way be mediated through causes. Instead, it can only be by induction—that is, by an increasing cumulative experience of the thing we are concerned to know about, that we may hope to win through eventually to an insight into or recognition of what the thing is essentially. And so it is in this sense and in this context that Aristotle chooses to characterize human sense perception as "a congenital discriminative capacity" which is the source of our human experience and thus of our human knowledge of the *what*'s of things. Not that an individual act of such perception—say, seeing a human being in front of me—is necessarily sufficient for a discernment and discrimination of what man is essentially. Rather it is from many such experiences that I can hope to induce the universal, or the nature or essence of man as such, that "one beside the many which is a single identity within them all."

So it is not merely with the induction of the *what* of man, but of other things as well. How is it that one learns what a triangle is as against a circle, or, on a still higher level of generality, what a certain kind of accident is—say that of quantity or of action—as contrasted to what substance is or what being is, or what change or motion is, or what happiness is, or the good life for man, etc.? In short, in all of these typically Aristotelian examples, and common-sense examples as well, is it not clear that it must be by some sort of induction from experience—which is simply to say by an eventual discernment of the one from among the many and of the essential as distinct from the accidental—that one achieves that very knowledge which is basic to all human knowledge—a knowledge of the very *what*'s or natures or essences of things?

The Divergence of Modern Logic
from Aristotelian Logic

If such, though, be the nature of induction, as Aristotle understands it, and if it be the function of such induction simply to vouchsafe to us a knowledge of things in terms of what they are, then it is little wonder that Aristotle's logic should not be receiving very high marks from very many of our contemporary philosophers and logicians today. For almost to a man these learned professors may be seen knowingly shaking their heads and, in their most condescending way, expressing their regrets over poor old Aristotle and his logic. The trouble, they would undoubtedly agree, is that while any such knowledge of the *what*'s and essences of things as

Aristotle would seem to call for might be all right if one could ever attain it, the fact is that it is unhappily and altogether unattainable —or at least unattainable by any such process of inference from experience as Aristotle called by the name of *induction.*

Nevertheless, before we re-enact the burial of Aristotle by modern philosophers on account of his partisanship for his favored procedure of *epagogê,* perhaps we ought first to consider how modern logic tends to diverge from Aristotle's logic not so much on the score of induction, as on that of purely formal and deductive logic as well. Already we have intimated in passing that modern logic is hardly to be regarded, in the way Aristotle regarded his logic, as merely the *organon* or instrument of human knowledge. Far from it. It is fashionable today, especially among formal logicians, to insist that logical and/or mathematical systems are in the strict sense purely formal systems, and hence wholly uninterpreted. By this they mean that the formulas of mathematics and of logic are made up wholly of variables, and the question of what the variables stand for, or even whether they stand for anything, is quite irrelevant to the formal rigor and completeness of the system. Instead, the system is determined simply on the basis of certain arbitrarily determined formation rules and transformation rules, as they are called.

Thus the formation rules would be mere stipulations to the effect that various kinds of wholly uninterpreted marks or symbols or sign designs were to be recognized as being the symbols in that system, and that these symbols may then be combined with one another to form a string of symbols only in certain rigorously prescribed ways. Accordingly, should any group or set of such symbols or sign designs be combined—once again, according to merely arbitrarily stipulated rules—then one could be said to have a well-formed expression of the system; otherwise, it would be an ill-formed expression. Analogously, too, with respect to the transformation rules: these rules simply prescribe the various ways in which it is permitted from one or more strings of symbols to derive other strings.

Clearly, though, in any system that is thus arbitrarily determined or set up in this way, it will be a concern wholly extrinsic to the system as to what the symbols of the system might stand for—whether for electric circuits, or chessmen, or playing cards, or quanta of energy, or geometrical figures, or logical devices like subject and predicates, or what not. But if the rules of the system have nothing necessarily to do with our human devices and instruments of knowledge, or with how such instruments need to be used if they are to yield knowledge, then it would hardly seem that a formal system, simply by virtue of being such, would have any sort of *prima facie* claim to being an *organon* of any kind, much less the *organon* of knowledge.

Be this as it may, as regards purely formal logical systems in the modern sense, the fact remains that various of these uninterpreted systems have been taken over by contemporary logicians and have been given interpretations that would seem to fit them for the role of a logical system, in the more narrowly Aristotelian sense of logic as the organon of knowledge. Thus suppose, for example, that certain of the symbols in a given uninterpreted system were to be given an interpretation such that these symbols might then represent subject variables, and still others predicate variables. Then the formation rules, in turn, might be so devised that when the signs were combined in the prescribed ways, the well-formed expressions would be more or less on the order of subject-predicate propositions of the kind that were the stock-in-trade of the older Aristotelian logic, and that, accordingly, might claim to be the sorts of logical devices that we must use if we are ever to come to a knowledge and understanding of things in terms of what they are.

Interestingly enough, even though Aristotelian logic in the

traditional sense might thus conceivably be set up as a purely formal system, and then interpreted in such a way as to yield an organon of the sort described, it is not this sort of thing that modern logicians would appear to have been interested in achieving at all. Or perhaps it might be more accurate to say that even if certain modern logicians might be considered to have been concerned with setting up systems that could be adapted for use as organs and instruments of knowledge, they nevertheless did not conceive that such an organon would be ordered to an understanding or knowledge of things in terms of what they are or why they are. No, rather than supposing that things were to be known in terms of what they are, it would seem as if modern logicians were bent on knowing things in terms of the possible relations that they might have to other things.

To give but a crude and overly simple illustration of this, one might say that various modern logicians—for instance, both Russell and Wittgenstein—at certain stages of their respective philosophical careers tended to think of reality, or the world, as being made up of individuals standing in countless different relations either to each other or to other entities in the world. Thus if we consider Socrates as such an individual for a moment, we might say "Socrates was the teacher of Plato," or "Socrates took the hemlock from the jailer," or "Socrates was snub-nosed." In the first such sentence one might say that what is being exhibited in the sentence is clearly a relationship (being the teacher of) between two individuals (Socrates and Plato). In fact, one might call '—— is the teacher of ——', a predicate with two subjects, or perhaps better, using Frege's terminology, a function with two arguments, and thus one might say that the first sentence above exhibits the following form or structure:

$$f(a,b)$$

Looking now at the third sentence, its structure would clearly seem to be that of a predicate with three subjects, or a function with three arguments. Thus the function is clearly "—— took —— from ——," and the three arguments in this case are Socrates, the hemlock, and the jailer. Again, schematically this might be exhibited as:

$$f(a,b,c)$$

And finally, the third of the above sentences considers Socrates, this time not in a relationship to another individual or even to other individuals, but rather in a relationship to a certain quality or a property as pertaining to him, snub-nosedness. Accordingly, the schematic representation of the structure of this sentence will be that of a function with only one argument:

$$f(a)$$

Arranging these sentences or propositional schemas in ascending order, then, we would come out with:

$$f(a)$$
$$f(a,b)$$
$$f(a,b,c)$$

The first we might simply designate as a one-place function, the second a two-place function, the third a three-place function. Nor need one stop there, but rather in principle one could go on to construct sentence-schemas of four-place, five-place, and so on up to n-place functions.

The Two Differing Conceptions As to
the Nature and Function of Logic

Now let us pause for a minute to compare this modern logical view of the structure of basic sentences or propositions with the Aristotelian view of the subject-predicate structure of such sentences and propositions. Superficially, the difference would seem to lie simply in the fact that Aristotle, apparently rather uncritically and arbitrarily, limited his basic sentences or propositions to one predicate and one subject each, whereas on the modern scheme the predicate or function term of a so-called elementary or atomic sentence need not be restricted to a single subject or argument, but rather may in principle have any number. What a marked gain this would seem to be, too, in that the modern scheme for such sentences and propositions would seem to be incredibly more flexible and extensible than the old straitjacket of the Aristotelian subject-predicate scheme!

Yet this difference is clearly only a superficial difference. For when one considers what the function or job is of sentences or propositions as conceived of according to the Aristotelian scheme, and what their function or job is conceived to be on the new scheme, the difference is much more far-reaching. As we have already seen, the job of an Aristotelian subject-predicate proposition is to make it possible for one to understand the subject under consideration in terms of what it is. Yet this is not at all the job or function of the sentence or proposition on the function-argument scheme. In fact, this latter way of conceiving of propositions is such as to make it quite impossible that through a proposition construed in this way one should ever come to an understanding of a thing in terms of what it is. Take the case of that two-place function which we considered above, "Socrates was the teacher of Plato." On the

Aristotelian interpretation, the predicate term is the entire notion of being-the-teacher-of-Plato; and when predicated of the one subject, "Socrates," what the proposition then signifies is what Socrates is or was accidentally. In contrast, on the modern interpretation of this same proposition as having two subjects, "Socrates" and "Plato," and one predicate "being the teacher of," one could hardly say that what Socrates and Plato were were teachers of. That makes no sense. No, the job of a sentence or proposition, construed according to the function-argument scheme, is not at all that of indicating or recognizing what something is, but rather that of indicating how one thing is related to another.

Moreover, even in the case of a one-place function as exemplified by the sentence "Socrates was snub-nosed," one must not suppose that on the new scheme the purpose or function of such a sentence is to indicate what Socrates is (or was); rather its purpose is to exhibit Socrates as standing in a certain relationship to one of his properties or attributes, that of snub-nosedness. After all, Socrates can no more be said to be the quality of snub-nosedness, than Socrates and Plato together could be said to be the relation teacher of. Furthermore, what Socrates is essentially is quite patently not a quality at all, but rather a substance. Likewise, what he is even only accidentally is never a quality as such. For one may not say—and that simply for the reason that one cannot think—that what Socrates is is but the quality of snub-nosedness. No, what one has to say is that Socrates is snub-nosed.

Accordingly, we can thus begin to see how and why, from the standpoint of the new logic, even in the case of a one-place function, the purpose or role of such a function is not to make possible the understanding of something in terms of what it is. Rather the purpose is to exhibit the relation that something stands in with respect to one of its qualities or attributes—in this particular instance the relation of Socrates to the quality or accident of snub-nosedness. So even in this last example our major contention would seem to be borne out: that in the new logic, even when a formal system that has been constructed according to the canons of such a logic is given an interpretation that might seem to enable it to function as a predicate calculus, or as a sentential calculus, and thus to be fitted for playing the role of the organon of knowledge, still the way in which it can then function as an organon must be quite different from the way in which Aristotle's logic was supposed to function as an organon. As we have seen, a subject-predicate sentence or proposition, as Aristotle conceives it, functions as an organon of knowledge precisely in the sense that it is a device conceived to enable us to understand things in terms of what they are. In contrast, the predicate calculus of the new logic is a device conceived to enable us to understand things in terms of their relationships to other things.

Moreover, this shift from a project for understanding things in terms of what they are to a project for understanding them in terms of their relations brings with it a further shift in what we might call the entire semantics of the new logic as contrasted with that of Aristotelian logic. If one asks the question as to how a so-called logic that is set up and conceived of primarily as a means for exhibiting possible schemas for different types of relations and relational structures is supposed to function as an organon of knowledge—just how is knowledge supposed to be mediated through and by means of relational schemas of the sort we have been considering—the answer that has been put forward by the non-Aristotelian logicians has tended to be two-fold, the second part being as it were a development out of, or perhaps even a reaction against, the first.

Thus, in the earlier days of the new logic, thinkers like Russell and Wittgenstein tended to suggest that the way in which the relational forms and schemas of the predicate calculus function as tools and instruments of knowledge is in virtue of their being able to represent or picture various corresponding relations or structures in the world. Thus in a celebrated and oft-quoted passage, Russell flatly says: "In a logically correct symbolism there will always be a certain fundamental identity of structure between a fact and the symbol for it. . . . [In short] there is an objective complexity in the world, and . . . it is mirrored by the complexity of propositions." [4] Even more specific by way of affirming that the way in which logical propositions and sentences are able to function as organs of knowledge is by virtue of their "picturing" the corresponding facts are the following pronouncements of Wittgenstein: "The picture is a model of reality. . . . That the elements of the picture are combined with one another in a definite way, represents that the things are so combined with one another. . . . [5] In order to be a picture a fact must have something in common with what it pictures. In the picture and the pictured there must be something identical in order that the one can be a picture of the other at all. What the picture must have in common with reality in order to be able to represent it after its manner—rightly or falsely—is its form of representation. The picture can represent every reality whose form it has." [6]

Now it hardly needs saying that such a picture theory of meaning is radically different from the sort of semantics that is to be associated with Aristotle's logic. If in an Aristotelian context one were to say that "A dog is an animal," one is certainly not supposing that dogs stand in a certain relationship to animals or to the character of animality, and that in the proposition the relation of *dog* to *animal* is therefore isomorphic with a supposed factual relationship in reality of dogs to animals, or even to animality. [7] Instead, what a thing is is not something which that thing stands over against and to which it may then be said to stand related in some particular way. Quite the contrary. In reality there is no separation of any kind of a thing from its own nature or essence, or from what it is. It is that we human beings, in our effort to understand things, will abstract a thing's own *what* from that thing itself and then in a logical proposition re-identify them by predicating the latter of the former. This is simply what understanding a thing in terms of what it is involves, and not any attempted picturing in which both picture and pictured are supposed to display a strict identity or isomorphism as regards their relational structure.

Needless to say, there are many things about such a picture theory of meaning as it came to be associated with the new logic in its earlier days that seemed disturbingly unsatisfactory. For one thing, from an Aristotelian point of view, such a semantic theory, so far from explaining how logic might serve as an organon or instrument of knowledge, seemed rather to beg the question of knowledge than to answer it. Stated bluntly, the criticism is that, given such a thing as a picture or photograph or for that matter any likeness or reproduction of another thing, the mere existence of such a likeness does not as such account for the fact that the thing of which it is a likeness should thereby come to be known. Rather it would seem to be the case that the picture itself must first come to be known. It must also come to be known and recognized precisely as a likeness. Otherwise, the picture or likeness, taken just in itself, would provide no leads at all as to what the likeness was supposed to be a likeness of. But how, in turn, is this prior knowledge of the picture or likeness itself to be understood, unless it be construed as being in some way or other a recognition of that picture or likeness for what it is?

But it is not this line of criticism which would seem to have led logicians and philosophers in more recent years to give up the picture theory of meaning altogether and to try to conceive quite differently the way in which the new logic may be understood as being an organon or instrument of knowledge. No, the source of the increasing doubts about the picture theory of meaning appear to have been a growing feeling that there is something radically wrong-headed about supposing that sentences or logical propositions are the kinds of things that ever are or can be put in a one-to-one correspondence with the corresponding facts. Thus Ryle spoke somewhat jestingly of the " 'Fido'–Fido theory," as he called it, and by this taunt he meant to suggest how foolish it was to suppose that for every word or name, "Fido," in a given sentence there must be a corresponding Fido in reality. Even Russell had made an earlier emphatic pronouncement to the effect that in so far as words like *or, and, if,* etc. are used in sentences, it cannot very well be supposed that there are real *or*s or *if*s or whatnot corresponding to them in reality.

But if a sentence or proposition is no longer supposed to be a vehicle of knowledge in virtue of its being an exact picture or likeness of the fact that it is supposed to provide a knowledge of, then in virtue of what will sentences and propositions be able to be vehicles or instruments of knowledge? Apparently, rather than return to anything like the Aristotelian theory according to which a proposition is a device for understanding things in terms of what they are, a great number of recent logicians and semanticists have resorted to a very different, not to say somewhat odd, tack. It is as if they had come simply to despair of ever being able to understand how through propositions and other logical devices one is ever to come to know things as they really are. Instead, they seem to be suggesting that what we should accustom ourselves to is to think of the relational structures of propositions not as picturing real relations between things as these are in fact and in reality, but rather as being simply our own human ways of relating and ordering and structuring the raw data of our experience. Not that things in themselves really are the way that we thus order and organize and put them together through our logical patterns and conceptual schemes; instead, the world as we know it—which is to say the world of science—is the way it is and has the character that it does have largely because we human beings have put it together in that way and have fashioned and constructed it according to the relational and structural patterns of our own logic. Needless to say, such a view of logic and of the peculiar role of logic in knowledge can trace its origins right back to Kant. But origins aside, in the present day the import of such a conception of logic is, indeed, to rehabilitate the notion of logic as being an organon, and perhaps even as an organon of knowledge. And yet it is not construed as being an organon of knowledge in the Aristotelian sense of being an instrument for disclosing or laying bare the nature of things as it really is in itself and independently of how we human beings construe or take it to be; rather it is an organon of knowledge in the sense of being that instrument through which we human beings, as it were, create our own world or at least fashion and structure it according to the ordering patterns and structuring relations of our own logic.

Induction Again: Is It the Source of the Supposed Irreconcilability of Modern Science with Aristotelian Philosophy?

Should the outcome of the preceding section seem strange, if not actually unsettling, need we add that this is hardly the time or occasion to undertake anything like a defense of the older Aristotelian conception of logic as an organon, as over against the newer and more lately in vogue conception of logic that we have just sketched out? Suffice it to say only that the two views of logic are indeed patently and radically different. Nevertheless, this newer and newly fashionable view of what might be called the distinctive semantic function and role of our present-day, non-Aristotelian logic may serve us as a means of shedding light on one final problem in regard to Aristotle's philosophy as a whole—a problem which we have really not touched upon directly in this book at all, and which yet must surely be in the back of the minds of all readers. For insofar as it has been our aim throughout this particular exposition of Aristotle's philosophy to try to present Aristotle as a contemporary philosopher, and as one who has something to say with respect to contemporary issues in philosophy; and even as one whose work is very much a live option that needs to be reckoned with on today's philosophical scene—still, for all of this, is it not obvious and inescapable that the immense and unavoidable stumbling block that any Aristotelian philosophy or version of Aristotle's philosophy simply cannot any longer get round is precisely the stumbling block of modern science? Historically, we have all been indoctrinated with accounts of Galileo's struggles against the Aristotelians of his day, and more generally we have simply come to take it for granted that, with respect to the entire rise and development of modern science, it was the Aristotelians who invariably seemed to be the leaders of the forces of obscurantism and reaction. Indeed, the very triumph of modern science has come to be viewed as having been no less than a function of the final and total defeat of Aristotelian philosophy.

Of course, it is easy enough to say, by way of making excuses for Aristotle, that he really had scarcely any notion of the tactics and procedures of scientific investigation as these have come to be practised and understood since the seventeenth century, and that when he wrote about physics, for example, it really wasn't physics in the modern sense that he was doing at all, but rather philosophy. Hence he perhaps ought not to be criticized for his inadequacies as a scientist, it being only as a philosopher that he ought to be judged. Such a line of defense in Aristotle's case, however, is unfortunately both insufficient and perhaps even misplaced. To take the example of physics again, it will be recalled that in our second chapter we pointed out that for Aristotle the physical universe is populated with the sorts of things he called *substances,* which substances, in turn, are composite of matter and form. But, alas, in modern physics when there is talk of matter, it is obviously not matter in Aristotle's sense at all. And when it comes to such things as the transfer between mass and energy, Aristotle's entire scheme of matter in relation to form and of potency in relation to act seems totally and utterly irrelevant. In fact, one might even say flatly that there is no evidence that there are any Aristotelian substances in physical nature at all. Or again, there are the more obvious examples of physical motion in general and of planetary motion in particular. The modern physicist will insist that motion is inertial in character, and not at all the sort of thing that Aristotle said it was. Or again, planetary motion, the modern scientist will say, has been shown to be in elliptical orbits, and not circular as Aristotle thought.

Now such differences and discrepancies, we shall be told, simply cannot be explained away merely on the ground that Aristotle was looking at things as a philosopher and not as a scientist. For in cases such as these Aristotle no less than the modern scientist would claim that it was empirical evidence that was the warrant for his assertions about physics and the physical universe. Yet clearly it would appear to be the case now that more and further evidence of the same empirical kind has been sufficient to show that Aristotle's inductions in the domain of physics—to recur again to the sort of logical procedure that is here involved— were inductions based on inadequate evidence, and hence have been superseded as a result of further research and are now to be discarded as simply false.

Plausible as all of this sounds, and accustomed as we all are simply to accept it as the standard historical account of how Aristotelian physics came to be displaced by modern physics, it is still possible that it may be both misleading and ill-conceived. In fact, we would like to suggest by way of concluding our account of Aristotelian philosophy that such issues as seem to divide Aristotle's physics from modern physics and modern science generally are really not issues, or ought not to be issues, as to the nature of things or of the physical world at all, but rather are logical issues in the broadest sense, the logic of modern science being, as it were, an entirely different logic from that which Aristotle used as his organon, and which, one might suggest, we all of us still continue to use simply as human beings in our everyday common-sense understanding of reality and of the world round about us.

Let us briefly consider the business of so-called induction, and whether it is indeed as a result of further inductions from experience that modern scientists have been led to throw out Aristotle's judgments about the nature of physical reality, replacing them with the more up-to-date judgments of modern physics. Already we have seen how Aristotle understands induction as being a process whereby from repeated experiences of things and events we are led to conclusions as to what they are essentially, and why they behave in the mode and manner in which they do. It was by inductions of this sort that Aristotle was convinced that he was led to an understanding of what things in the sense of physical substances were, and how they differed from so-called accidents like quantity, quality, relation, action, passion, etc.; how they were subject to changes of various kinds; and why, being thus subject to change, they were necessarily composite of form and matter; what change itself was, and why it necessarily involved the three principles of being always a change of something, to something, and from something, etc.

Shifting, then, to the modern scientific scene, we would suggest that it is not by inductions at all—at least not by inductions from experience in Aristotle's sense—that the modern scientist has arrived at his very different conclusions about the physical world. For one thing, we all know that when a scientist, particularly a physical scientist, talks about his data, he apparently hardly means the same thing as what we as human beings mean when we talk about our experience or experiences. For human experience is quite patently an experience of such things as tables and chairs, of men and mice, of night and day, of summer and winter, of man's folly and misery, etc. But a physicist's data do not include human experiences of this sort at all; rather they are things such as pointer readings, impressions on a photographic plate, etc.; in fact, one might say that they are all ultimately reducible to the sorts of things that Hume called sense impressions, or that more recent philosophers have called sense data—namely, mere momentary sensed events like flashes of light, patches of color, passing shapes and configurations, sounds of varying pitches and loudness, etc. In other words, if we were to use Aristotle's terminology, we might say that the only data which the modern scientist will accept, by and large, are the mere data of the so-called external senses, of sight, of touch, of hearing, etc.; but these do not include any of the things which Aristotle spoke of as being "sensed by accident"—the substances that have the colors and shapes, that are rough or smooth to the touch, that emit the sounds, that have such and such quantitative dimensions, etc.

But from mere data such as these, and to the exclusion of anything and everything that as Aristotle would say can be sensed by accident, it is obvious that one cannot make any inductions either as to what things are or why they are—at least not in the sense of what one would ordinarily take these expressions to mean. Thus, to take a crude and trivial example, Aristotle felt that from our experience of human beings, we can by induction come to recognize what men are essentially—rational animals, or organic bodies informed by a rational soul. But contrast a modern behavioristic psychologist: he might very well say that as a scientist he feels warranted in doing no more than to uncover and take cognizance of all the incredibly varied stimulus-response patterns as they pertain to a so-called human organism; but as to what such an organism is essentially, or what its substantial form is—as to this sort of thing, he would say that he is just not qualified to speak at all, and perhaps that he would even consider the very questions to be meaningless when put to him in his capacity as a scientist. For that matter, even as regards the specific patterns of stimulus and response, if one were to ask the psychologist why it is that the organism should respond in the particular way it does to those particular stimuli, he would probably reply in much the same vein as Hume: *that* there is a recurring correlation of stimulus *a* with response *b*, he would insist that he has evidence for; but as to *why a* should thus be correlated with *b*, he would doubtless say that he simply does not know.

To cut this matter short, may we not say that given the peculiar kinds of empirical procedures that are practised in contemporary science, there not only are not, but there cannot be, any inductions as to the *what*'s or *why*'s of things. This having come to be quite generally recognized, if not by the scientists themselves, then certainly by philosophers of science in the present day, one now finds it put forward as almost a common-place among contemporary philosophers of science that induction plays no major role in science at all any more. In fact, rather than to suppose that scientific hypotheses or scientific theories are in any way derived from the data of observation, either by induction or by any other logical means, one finds a philosopher of science like the eminent Sir Karl Popper insisting that scientists, so far from basing their hypotheses on the data, simply make them up out of whole cloth! In fact, one even hears it said that the invention of scientific theories, so far from being anything that is guided by a regard for the facts or the data of observation, is to be compared with the composing of a symphony, or the devising of a plot for a novel. True, it is still for the most part recognized that scientific theories and hypotheses are subject to a control by the data of observation, at least to the extent that if they are not in conformity with the data, then they may be considered to have been falsified, and so may be thrown out. And yet there are some among the more radical of latter-day philosophers of science, men like Hanson, Kuhn, and Feyerabend, who would go so far as to say that as scientific theories and hypotheses may not be considered to be based on empirical data in any way, so also they cannot even be said to be falsifiable by the data of observation—at least not in any unequivocal way.

But whether one goes quite as far as to say that contemporary scientific pronouncements about the nature of the physical universe are neither induced from empirical evidence, nor even controlled by such evidence in any unequivocal way, still the problem does remain as to what possible warrant or justification there can be for scientific pronouncements if it is no longer possible to regard them as being based on inductions from experience. With this question we find ourselves being carried back once more to those same logical considerations which were raised in the preceding sections. There we found that many modern logicians, having given up the idea that logical relations can ever picture the facts, have tended to go to the opposite extreme of supposing that logical relations, instead of mirroring the structure of the facts, are rather to be regarded as actually constituting and even creating the structures which the facts have come to have, if not in themselves, then at least for us.

With this, though, there would seem to be suggested at least a possible line of justification for scientific statements and theories as to the nature of the physical world. It is the kind of justification that Kant would have called a transcendental justification, and roughly it follows the pattern that we have seen emerging in connection with the semantics of modern logic. For if the theories of modern science are not based on the facts of experience and really do not reflect them at all, then perhaps these theories, so far from representing the way things really are in the physical world, reflect instead only the ways in which we have come to view the physical world, the ways we take it to be, and thus the ways in which it is for us. In other words, physical nature appears to the scientist not at all in the way in which it is in itself, but only as it is patterned and structured and organized and put together according to the ordering principles which his logic imposes upon it.

And what might the consequences of all this then be, so far as the status and validity of Aristotle's physics, and indeed of his philosophy as a whole, are concerned? Surely, the consequence would be to leave it all standing pretty much intact. For the logic by which Aristotle reaches his account of being and of the nature of things may now be seen to be an entirely different logic from that which is operative in modern science. Moreover, not only is it a different logic, but the very kind of knowledge that is mediated by the one sort of logical organon is quite different from that of the other: in the one case the knowledge is a knowledge of being and of things as they are in themselves; in the other case the knowledge is not a knowledge of being or of the nature of things or of the way things are in the usual sense at all, but only of the way things are for us, and of being as it appears to us when structured by the logical forms and patterns which we impose upon it in our efforts to know it and deal with it.

Why, then, may we not say that Aristotle's inductions and his knowledge of things in terms of what they are and why they are are in general perfectly sound: the evidence for them is cogent and, as we have had repeated occasion to observe, the judgments which he makes and the conclusions which he draws from the evidence are such as we ourselves find quite undeniable when we consider them simply from the point of view of our common sense as human beings. At the same time, the sort of philosophical knowledge which one is thus able to attain of nature and of the nature of change, of human nature and of the good life, of being *qua* being, etc.—nearly all of this knowledge which is vouchsafed to us if we follow Aristotle's lead tends to be a knowledge that is of a very high order of generality, and that scarcely penetrates to specific and concrete details of the myriad facts and events of reality.

To recur just briefly to a single example that we have already noted earlier, may we not say that while Aristotle's general account of change and of the causes of change is not only one that makes sense, but even one that seems undeniable to our common sense, still when it comes to the business of calculating the exact speed and distance of a particular moving body like that of a projectile, say, or of the rate of descent of a freely falling body, for instance—then it is true that Aristotle's general account no longer suffices for such purposes. Instead, we have need to make a shift in the very logic that we use; and instead of an Aristotelian logic that is an organon for knowing the *what*'s and *why*'s of things as they really are, we must make do with that radically different type of logic which is the organon of science, and according to which we are enabled to view things and to take them in certain ways as patterned after our own conceptual schemes and logical relations which we ourselves have imposed upon things, and by virtue of which we are able to calculate and manipulate things as they are for us and as they appear to us with an incredible efficacy and efficiency both.

Considering, therefore, the respective logics which they would thus seem to employ, surely there would seem to be no reason why an Aristotelian philosophy might not be entirely reconcilable with a modern science. And given this state of affairs with respect to the relations between science and philosophy, there is surely no reason that Aristotle should not once again be considered to be a truly live option in philosophy—and perhaps not merely a live option, but even the only option open to a man of a healthy common sense with respect to the realities of things generally and of our human situation particularly.

Further Readings
in and about Aristotle

"Hope springs eternal in the human breast"—and so, given any sort of initial interest or curiosity regarding Aristotle, the neophyte and general reader is likely to turn with hope to the texts of Aristotle, only to put them down again disconsolately, perhaps sorrowfully completing the quotation, "Man never is, but always to be blessed"!

There are, however, translations of Aristotle, which, though they can hardly guarantee that the reader will be blessed with coveted understanding of the philosopher, can nevertheless be looked into with the assurance of their having been executed with scholarship, being generally reliable, and moderately intelligible. First in this connection should be mentioned the many-volumed standard Oxford translations of *The Works of Aristotle*, under the editorship of W. D. Ross and published by the Clarendon Press. Perhaps, too, the Aristotle volumes in the Loeb Classical Library, now published by the Harvard University Press, should be mentioned. These latter have the great advantage of having the Greek text printed on the one page and the English translation on the facing page. Of these various Loeb translations, the ones doubtless deserving particular mention are those of the *Ethics* and the *Politics* by H. Rackham. Also there is the unusual and even somewhat fulsome translation of the *Physics* by P. H. Wicksteed and revised by F. M. Cornford. The notes and introductory summaries in these two volumes are often invaluable. Leaving the Loeb Library translations, at least passing reference might be made to H. G. Apostle's translation (Indiana University Press) of the *Metaphysics*, perhaps the most difficult of Aristotle's works. Nor is it entirely gratuitous to remark on the singularly felicitous French translations of the major works of Aristotle by J. Tricot and published by Joseph Vrin in Paris. The merit of these translations lies simply in that, far from regarding Aristotle's texts as just so much ancient Greek that calls for a scholar's rendering into a modern language, the translator seems to have made the very novel and refreshing assumption that what Aristotle is saying does indeed make genuine philosophical sense, which it is the primary business of the translator to try to convey to the reader of the translation. Besides, the notes printed at the bottom of the page are almost entirely free of the usual scholarly lumber and are aimed precisely at trying to shed philosophical light on the particular points that Aristotle happens to be engaged in struggling with and breaking his head over.

Passing from translations to commentaries, there are literally mountains of them that have been accumulating from Aristotle's time right down to the present, and that for the most part reflect a pattern of voluminousness that can be nothing if not disheartening to the general reader. From the Middle Ages there might be singled out the commentaries of St. Thomas Aquinas on the *Metaphysics*, the *Physics*, the *De Anima*, and the *Ethics* (to mention the more obvious ones). These have all been translated into English, and might well be profitably consulted, particularly since they are exceedingly luminous in places. The trouble is to find those places! Of modern commentaries in English, custom requires that respect be paid to the painstaking scholarship of W. D. Ross who prepared editions and commentaries of the *Metaphysics*, *Physics*, *De Anima*, *Parva Naturalia*, and *Prior and Posterior Analytics*, all published by Oxford. Unfortunately, Ross's depressingly exhaustive scholarship tends to smother the interest of philosopher and general reader alike. One contemporary commentary that does merit a more enthusiastic mention, however, is the incomparable study of the *Metaphysics* by the Rev. Joseph Owens, entitled *The Doctrine of Being in the Aristotelian Metaphysics* (2nd edn., Pontifical Institute of Mediaeval Studies, Toronto, 1957). This book is not easy reading, but it is incalculably rich and rewarding.

Enough, then, of commentaries, and to come to what might be called more general studies of Aristotle and his philosophy—studies that, unhappily, might be roughly comparable in intent and purpose to this present book, but that may be judged to have brought the job off rather more successfully. Of course, any man's listing of his competitors is bound to be suspect, and particularly when they are philosopher-competitors. Besides, any act of selection of a few titles from the bewildering array of contemporary studies on Aristotle can hardly fail to seem at once arbitrary and gratuitous. For better or for worse, however, mention might be made of the following:

Marjorie Grene, *A Portrait of Aristotle*, Chicago: The University of Chicago Press, 1963. This is an exceedingly readable and illuminating presentation of Aristotle's philosophy. Justly praised for its attempt to understand Aristotle against the background of his interest in biology, the book is also excellent for its apt reflection of the pervasive influence on his thought of Aristotle's logic—that is, of logic in Aristotle's sense, not in the modern sense.

John Wild, *An Introduction to Realistic Philosophy*, New York: Harper and Brothers, 1948. This book was written as an introductory textbook in philosophy, but it attempts to accomplish its purpose by being a superb introduction to Aristotle. Unfortunately, the book is marred by an opening chapter which argues most ineptly for the superiority of Aristotle over any and all modern philosophers! However, in Part I a most lucid and plausible exposition is given of Aristotle's ethics and politics, and in Part II of his physics and psychology.

W. D. Ross, *Aristotle*, London: Methuen, 5th edition 1956. It is nearly fifty years since the first edition of this work by the great classical scholar and expert on Aristotle. Described by a reviewer as "a masterpiece of condensed exposition," the book is just that, except that the condensation is such as to make the philosophical import of Aristotle almost completely indiscernible in its pages.

G. E. M. Anscombe, "Aristotle: the Search for Substance" in Anscombe and Geach, *Three Philosophers*, Oxford: Blackwell, 1961.

This is a study of Aristotle by an eminent contemporary English philosopher. It is difficult reading, but very suggestive. Unfortunately, one is perhaps never too sure whether the search for substance at Professor Anscombe's hands ever does culminate in anything like an unequivocal disclosure of the thing searched for.

One final regret and apology. In these bibliographical remarks, no references have been made to various excellent studies of particular departments or divisions of Aristotle's thought, such as the ethics, the politics, the poetics, the psychology etc. But of books on Aristotle the list could easily become unending, so that a line must be drawn somewhere, if only to spare author and reader alike. μηδὲν ἄγαν!

Notes

Chapter I

1. Ernest Barker, *The Politics of Aristotle* (Oxford: *At the Clarendon Press*, 1946), p. xiv.

2. Bertrand Russell, *Selected Papers of Bertrand Russell* (New York: The Modern Library, n.d.), pp. 352–353.

3. At this point it would be easy to cavil, and to say that Aristotle would never have appealed to any such thing as "the common sense of mankind." For one thing, like his fellow Greeks he would certainly have made a well-nigh absolute distinction between Greeks and barbarians; and that anything like the common sense of mankind could properly be ascribed to mere barbarians, any Greek would probably have doubted. Besides, nowhere in Aristotle's writings is there found any explicit or developed doctrine of common sense, in the sense in which we are using the term. For all of this, though, we feel it to be a not improper interpretive principle to read Aristotle as being just the kind of philosopher who does not hesitate to make at least implicit appeal to what we have rather loosely termed the commonsense judgment of human kind.

4. The description is actually Russell's in one of the essays in *Mysticism and Logic*, quoted from Charles A. Fritz, *Bertrand Russell's*

Construction of the External World (New York: The Humanities Press, 1952), p. 139.

Chapter II

1. W. R. Thompson, *Science and Common Sense* (London: Longmans Green and Co., 1937), pp. 57–58.

2. *Selected Papers of Bertrand Russell*, pp. 355–356.

3. This label is perhaps infelicitous. For while Zeno might be said to have set forth a view of change as mere succession, he did not himself necessarily subscribe to it.

Chapter III

1. Aristotle, *De Anima* II, 1, 412b 9–15.

2. Ibid., 412b 19–20.

3. *De Anima* II, 4, 415b 7–11. (Oxford translation slightly altered and emended.)

4. Cf. *Physics* VIII, 254b 33–255a 5.

5. Doubtless, it should be explained that we are not using this word here in its current everyday sense, but rather in its Scholastic sense derived from the technical term, *intentio,* in Scholastic Latin. In this latter sense, an "intention" signifies simply a tending of the mind or cognitive faculty toward that which thereby comes to be known or is the object of such knowledge.

6. Cf. *De Anima* III, 2.

7. *De Anima* III, 4, 429a, 27–28.

8. Cf. the distressingly abbreviated account in *De Anima* III, 5.

9. Ibid., 430a 23–26.

Chapter IV

1. Cf. Aristotle *The Nicomachean Ethics* VI, 2, 1139a, 21–25.

2. Ibid., 1139a, 26–31. We have quoted from Rackham's translation in the Loeb Library with slight alterations and emendations.

3. Ibid., 1139a, 7–9.

4. Ibid., 1104a, 2–10. Cf. 1094b, 12–27.

5. Ibid., 1097b, 21–23.

6. Ibid., 1097b, 25–1098a 4.

7. Jean-Paul Sartre, *Existentialism*, trans. by Bernard Frechtman (New York: Philosophical Library, 1947), pp. 28–30.

8. Ibid., p. 31.

9. Ibid., pp. 32–33.

10. Aristotle, *The Politics*, I, 1, 1253a 3.

11. Ibid.

12. *The Nicomachean Ethics*, X, 7, 1177b 18–21. (Loeb Library, Rackham translation.)

13. Ibid., 1177b 26–1178a 18–21.

Chapter V

1. That is to say, all of these various sciences represent but so many applications and specifications of those basic notions and principles which

we have already encountered in Aristotle's physics—*e.g.,* substance and accident, matter and form, potency and act, the four causes, etc.

2. For example, in *Metaphysics* E. ch. 1. Be it noted, however, that *metaphysics* is not the term that Aristotle himself uses either in this particular passage or any other. Rather his term is either *first philosophy* or *theology.* As to the explanation of this latter term, we shall have more to say presently.

3. Aristotle would call them *theoretical sciences,* as distinguished from practical or productive sciences.

4. Need we be reminded that all of the various sciences, as we know them today, have as a matter of historical fact developed out of the subject that was traditionally known as natural philosophy, or "physics" in Aristotle's sense?

5. The most recent scholarly opinion would now seem to frown upon this long-held view. Cf. Joseph Owens, *The Doctrine of Being in the Aristotelian Metaphysics* (Toronto: The Pontifical Institute of Mediaeval Studies, 2nd edition, 1963), p. 74.

6. This word which one sometimes finds in the literature today must give offense to purists, combining as it does a Latin prefix with a Greek root. However, *metaempirical* has never caught on, and hence does not convey the needed sense.

7. *Metaphysics*, Z., ch. 2, 1028b 3–4.

8. This assumes, of course, that Plato's Forms are to be interpreted not as being present in particulars, but rather as being the sorts of things that particulars participate in.

9. For this term itself, as well as for a masterly exposition of the entire doctrine which it is meant to designate, we are indebted to Father Owens' book, op. cit., v, especially chapters 1 and 3. Literally translated, *pros hen* means "with respect to one" or "with reference to one."

10. *Metaphysics*, Z., ch. 2, 1003a 33–b18, (Oxford translation).

11. This word is used here simply in the sense of "not-predicable," and not in the somewhat technical sense that has been given to it in the context of certain discussions in modern logic.

12. *Metaphysics*, 1028b 3–4.

13. Cf. *Metaphysics*, Z, ch. 3.

14. By way of further apology we might say that our treatment will not only be cursory, but also somehwat tendentious in that we shall present a highly simplified rendering of the sort of argument Aristotle gives for god's existence; nor shall we be too scrupulous about distinguishing sharply between a properly Aristotelian type of argument to this effect and later Scholastic arguments.

15. *Metaphysics*, 1074b, 34.

16. One might object, and perhaps rightly so, that Aristotle would never have concerned himself with arguing for an ultimate cause that would account for the being or existence either of the world or of the things in the world. Instead, his ultimate causes were never more than causes designed to provide an explanation of the changes or motions that are going on in the world and have been going on eternally. All the same, even if it be somewhat tendentious, we think it not a serious misrepresentation of Aristotle to suggest that the basic thrust of his philosophy is certainly one that would call for a metaphysics by way of a supplement to what in the present day might be called a mere ontology.

17. On this whole issue, cf. Owens, op. cit., esp. chs. 1 and 3.

18. *Metaphysics*, E, ch. 1, 1026a 24–33. The translation used is that of H. G. Apostle, *Aristotle's Metaphysics* (Bloomington: Indiana University Press, 1966), stress added.

Chapter VI

1. *Immanuel Kant's Critique of Pure Reason*, trans. by Norman Kemp Smith (London: Macmillan and Co., 1929), B VIII.

2. It should be noted that although the familiar schema "S is P" has become traditional in so-called Aristotelian logic, Aristotle himself tended not to exhibit the structure of propositions in quite that way. Rather than "S is P," he seemed to prefer the locution, "P belongs to S." Now in the eyes of some present-day logicians this is a matter of no little significance. Indeed, on the strength of it, they have sometimes been wont to say that what has come to be known in the history of Western philosophy as "Aristotelian logic" is something quite different from Aristotle's own logic. This particular issue of present-day Aristotelian scholarship, however, is surely one that we may be permitted to pass over in silence.

3. Aristotle, *Analytica Posteriora*, Book II, ch. 19, 99b 34–100b 5. (Oxford translation). Cf. *Metaphysica*, Book A, ch, 1.

4. Bertrand Russell, "The Philosophy of Logical Atomism," in *Logic and Knowledge*, ed. by Marsh (New York: The Macmillan Company, 1956), p. 197.

5. Ludwig Wittgenstein, *Tractatus Logico-Philosophicus* (London: Kegan Paul, Trench, Trubner and Co., 3rd impression, 1947), p. 39 (2.12 and 2.15).

6. Ibid., p. 41 (2.16–2.17).

7. This is not to imply that, as regards this particular example, either Russell or Wittgenstein would suppose that there was any simple isomorphism between proposition and fact.

Index